SIMPLE ARABIC

Yousif Haddad and Jack Ingle

SIMPLE ARABIC
A Comprehensive Course

Saqi Books

British Library Cataloguing-in-Publication Data
A catalogue record for this book is available from the
British Library

ISBN 0 86356 757 6 (hb)
ISBN 0 86356 342 2 (pb)

Saqi Books
26 Westbourne Grove
London W2 5RH
www.saqibooks.com

Dedicated to the memory of
Irene and Nigel

CONTENTS

PREFACE

This guide is intended to serve the needs of those whose aim is to write in Arabic or to read Arabic books and newspapers. It has been written in *Modern Standard Arabic,* avoiding the use of most colloquial words and expressions, by an English student and an Arab teacher who have brought their own different perspectives to bear on the subject. The book may be used in self-directed study or it may equally be used in a conventional classroom situation.

Much of the material included in this book has been taught for many years by Dr. Haddad and is primarily aimed at the student of Arabic who has already gained some basic knowledge of the language, and as transliteration has not been used, one who is able to read Arabic script (although this is not a prerequisite). In order to assist the student, all the Arabic letters and signs have been summarized at the beginning of the book.

Although there are a number of different textbooks available in varying formats, this guide is intended to consolidate and extend the range of *modern* grammar and ancillary topics, in a clear and concise way that is both easy to read and easy to assimilate.

The units have been condensed to the essentials of each topic, and all the linguistic structures required for GCSE Arabic and beyond have been covered. As the book has been comprehensively indexed in both languages, it makes an ideal reference work to revise for examinations or simply to quickly refresh one's memory on a specific point.

The words used in this book were selected on the basis of frequency of use in contemporary Arabic.

LIST OF ABBREVIATIONS

acc.	accusative
adj.	adjective
c.	about
coll.	collective
colloq.	colloquial
d	dual
e.g.	for example
f	feminine
fp	feminine plural
fs	feminine singular
gen.	genitive
i.e.	that is
lit.	literally
m	masculine
mp	masculine plural
ms	masculine singular
nom.	nominative
p	plural
s	singular
sfp	sound feminine plural
smp	sound masculine plural
viz.	namely (videlicet)

The Arabic Alphabet حُرُوفُ الهِجَاءِ

Names of Letters		Letters	Transliteration	Sun (S)/Moon (M)
أَلِف	alif	ا	a	M
باء	baa'	ب	b	M
تاء	taa'	ت	t	S
ثاء	thaa'	ث	th	S
جيم	jiim	ج	j	M
حاء	Haa'	ح	H	M
خاء	khaa'	خ	kh	M
دال	daal	د	d	S
ذال	dhaal	ذ	dh	S
راء	raa'	ر	r	S
زاي	zaay	ز	z	S
سين	siin	س	s	S
شين	shiin	ش	sh	S
صاد	Saad	ص	S	S
ضاد	Daad	ض	D	S
طاء	Taa'	ط	T	S
ظاء	DHaa'	ظ	DH	S
عَيْن	:ayn	ع	:	M
غَيْن	ghayn	غ	gh	M
فاء	faa'	ف	f	M
قاف	qaaf	ق	q	M
كاف	kaaf	ك	k	M
لام	laam	ل	l	S

ميم	miim	م	m	M
نون	nuun	ن	n	S
هاء	haa'	ه	h	M
واو	waaw	و	w	M
ياء	yaa'	ي	y	M
هَمْزَة	hamza	ء	'	M

«ا» ـ أَلِف alif

This letter has several functions within the Arabic alphabet. The main ones are:

(a) It acts as a carrier for the هَمْزَة and the sign مَدَّة ـ آ (see below).

(b) It acts as a long vowel (see paragraph on **vowels** below).

(c) It is added at the end of *indefinite* words in the **accusative case** to accompany the - **an** sound nunation unless the word ends in certain letters (see Unit 3: Cases).

(d) It occurs at the end of foreign nouns which end in a long -**aa** sound:

England إنكلترا Russia روسيا America أميركا pasha باشا

(e) It occurs at the end of certain parts of the Arabic verb (see Units: 12, 13 and 14).

«ء» ـ هَمْزَة hamza

There are two types of *hamza:* (a) the joining *hamza;* and (b) the cutting *hamza.*

The Joining Hamza (هَمْزَةُ الوَصْلِ)
This is shown by a special sign called وَصْلَة and is written over the *alif* of words beginning with «ال» or «ا». It is only of significance in connected speech and is rarely shown in modern written Arabic. The sign is not shown in this book.

The Cutting Hamza (هَمْزَةُ القَطْعِ)
This orthographic sign, which gives the glottal stop sound, can occur in any

position in a word and is usually carried on any of the letters *alif, waaw* or *yaa',* **or,** it may be positioned without a carrier.

Where the *hamza* is placed in a word defines the way it is written:

رأي، سؤال، عائلة، شاطئ، شيء، ضوء، هواء

At the **beginning** of a word it **must** be carried on an «ا». It is written over the *alif* when it takes an **-a** vowel or **-u** vowel but it is written below the *alif* when it takes an **-i** vowel:

أَرض   أُسبوع،   إِذا،

In the **middle** it can be carried on one of the three long vowels:

سأل   بدؤوا،   رئيس،

At the **end** of a word it may **stand alone** - شتاء or be **carried by any of the long vowels**:

بدأ   بطؤَ،   برئَ،

Notes
1. The *hamza* takes the short vowels and the *sukuun* like any other consonant in the Arabic alphabet.
2. The *yaa'* when written with a *hamza* loses its two dots: شاطئ (see ألف مقصورة on p.17).

«ة» ـ تَاء مَرْبُوطَة

This hybrid, usually denoting a feminine word, *only* appears in the *final* position of a word and does not have its own individual sound. It uses the preceding **-a** vowel sound:

lady سيِّدَة   *star* نجمَة

When the letter is followed by a **pronoun suffix** it is pronounced as a **-t** and written as an ordinary «ت»:

newspaper جريدَة   *your [mp] newspaper* جريدَتكم

It is also pronounced as a **-t** if the noun is the property element in a possessive construction:

Mubarak's ball كُرَة مبارك

If a case ending is put on the word it is pronounced as a **-t**.

The Vowels

In written Arabic there are three recognized vowels which occur in short and long forms.

Short Vowels الحَرَكَات

These vowels have shortened forms which are placed above or below the consonants.

1. The **-a** vowel is shown by a (́) فَتْحَة and is placed above the consonant:

    he wrote كَتَبَ

2. The **-u** vowel is shown by a (́) ضَمَّة and is placed above the consonant:

    books كُتُب

3. The **-i** vowel is shown by a (̣) كَسْرَة and is placed below the consonant:

    years سِنِين

The three short vowels are shown together in the word عُلِمَ *it is learnt*

The short vowels are not usually shown in modern written Arabic.

Long Vowels حُرُوف المَدّ [lit. Letters of Prolongation]

The three short vowels have lengthened forms (ي و ا).

They are pronounced as: ا **-aa**   و **-uu**   ي **-ii**

                    people نَاس   *light* نُور   *in* فِي

In a vowelled text the short vowels are shown in combination with the letters ي و ا

Note that the three long vowels are more extended when they occur in the middle of a word than when they are in a final position.

Diphthongs

In addition to the above vowels there are **two** diphthongs in Arabic (وَ and يَ). These are also written without the short vowels and in addition *maintain* their consonant sounds.

They are pronounced as: وَ -aw   يَ -ay
نَوْع *type, sort*   زَيْت *oil*

٥ ـ سُكُون *sukuun*

This sign is used to show that *no vowel* follows a consonant:

عِنْد *by, with*

ّ ـ شَدَّة *shadda*

This sign is used to *double a consonant* and is written over the letter:

جدّة *grandmother*   سلّة *basket*

It is important to take care in its pronunciation as lengthening the consonant creates a different meaning, especially in relation to verbs:

كَسَّرَ *he smashed*   كَسَرَ *he broke*   دَرَّسَ *he taught*   دَرَسَ *he studied*

آ» ـ مَدَّة *madda*

This sign is pronounced as an extra-long أَلِف and comprises آ = ا + أَ:

آنسة *Miss (lady)*   القُرآن *Quran*   الآن *now*   آلاف *thousands*

«ى» ـ أَلِف مَقْصُورَة

Some words that end in a long -aa vowel are written with a *yaa'* with the two dots omitted (ى) instead of an *alif*. This is known as ألف مقصورة or ألف. The ألف مقصورة occurs only at the end of a word and is pronounced the same as an *alif*.

Examples:

Verbs   إشترى *he bought*   رأى *he saw*   أعطى *he gave*

17

Nouns	wealth	غِنـى	young man	فَتى	before noon ضُحى
Particles	until	حتّى	on	على	to إلى
Proper nouns or names	مصطفى		عيسى		موسى

Dagger "*alif*" أَلِف

This an أَلِف, producing the long -aa sound, which in classical Arabic is shown as a vertical sign over a letter. This is *not* shown in modern Arabic but is *always* pronounced. This sign can occur over a letter in an initial or medial position and must be remembered. In **ex. 1-5** it is placed above the first letter, and in **ex. 1** it is placed above the *shadda* of the second «ل»:

1. اللّه   2. هَذين   3. هَؤُلاء   4. ذَلك   5. هَذه   6. هَذا

Mention of this sign is made in the various units where appropriate.

Note

There is no universal convention on printing throughout the Arab world. The letter ي at the end of words is often printed without its two dots, i.e. ى. This can lead to its being mistaken for an ألف مقصورة. The short vowels, the *shadda* and the *sukuun* are not usually shown in modern print. This unfortunately can cause confusion to students of the language.

Throughout the following units the small vowels and orthographic signs have been shown only to aid comprehension and to illustrate grammatical points where necessary, at the authors' discretion. As few signs are used in modern Arabic, the student must quickly adapt to reading the language without them.

INDEFINITE AND DEFINITE النَّكِرَةُ والمَعْرِفَةُ

There is no indefinite article in Arabic corresponding to the English **"a"** or **"an"**. The absence of the definite article denotes *"indefiniteness"*.

The Definite Article (ال) أداة التَّعْريف

The article is joined to the noun or the adjective it defines and is considered an integral part of that word, and not two separate words as English:

a book كتاب   *the book* الكتاب

With the addition of the definite article (ال) the Arabic alphabet is linguistically divided into **sun (S)** letters (الحُروف الشَّمْسِيَّة) and **moon (M)** letters (الحُروف القَمَرِيَّة).

The **sun** letters affect the pronunciation of the definite article, i.e. the (ل) of the article is dropped in pronunciation and the following **sun** letter is *doubled*. This is shown by the «ّ» over the **sun** letter and the operation is called تَشْديد:

a *moon*	قَمَر	pronounced	*qamar*
the moon	القَمَر	pronounced	*al qamar*
a *sun*	شَمْس	pronounced	*shams*
the sun	الشَّمْس	pronounced	*ash-shams*

Use of the Definite Article

Arabic uses the definite article in a number of situations where English does not. These include:

1. With **abstract nouns** when used in a general sense:

    Faithfulness is a virtue   الوفاء فضيلة

    Love is blind   الحبّ أعمى

    Necessity is the mother of invention   الحاجة أُمّ الإختراع

2. With **names of materials** which cannot be counted and therefore have *no plurals*:

iron حديد   gold ذهب   milk حليب

Gold is dearer than copper   الذَّهب أغلى مِن النُّحاس

3. With **languages** and other **academic subjects**:

He studies Arabic and history   يدرس العربيّة والتَّاريخ

4. In **expressions**, particularly adverbial ones:

from morning till evening   مِن الصَّباح إلى المساء

from beginning to end   مِن البداية إلى النِّهاية

night and day   في اللَّيل والنَّهار

5. In phrases referring to **life**:

Life is sweet   الحياة حلوة

happiness in life   السَّعادة في الحياة

public life   الحياة العامّة

Genitive Construction إِضَافَة: المُضَافُ والمُضَافُ إِلَيْهِ

There are two parts to a *genitive construction:* a) the property; and b) the owner.

In essence a *genitive construction* إضافة consists of two elements: *the first,* the governing noun, is the **construct** المضاف, and *the second* المضاف إليه is the **genitive**. The relationship between these two elements is illustrated and discussed below.

The *first element* of a genitive construction, also referred to as a possessive construction, **is always a noun**, while the *second element* **can be a noun or a pronoun suffix**.

In **English** we express possession in the following way: *owner* then *property*:

the student's book or *John's house*

In **Arabic** the construction is reversed and is **always: *property* then *owner*:**

1. *the student's book*   كتابُ الطَّالبِ

2. *the manager of the company*   مديرُ الشَّركةِ

3. *the house of Noori*   بيتُ نوري

4. *Rafidayn Bank*   بنكُ الرَّافِدَيْنِ

5. *the Minister of Defence*   وزيرُ الدِّفاع

6. *the girl's singing*   غناءُ البنتِ

7. *the writing of letters*   كتابةُ الرَّسائلِ

8. *the driver of the car*   سائقُ السَّيَّارةِ

The relationship between the two elements of a *construct phrase* in Arabic goes beyond that of *property and owner*. They are related in a variety of ways which include:

    action/doer (ex. 6), *action/object* (ex. 7) and *doer/object* (ex. 8).

Notes

1. The **first noun** *(property)*, although it has no definite article attached to it, becomes *definite* by coupling it with the **second noun** *(owner)* in a possessive construction and **loses its nunation** (see Unit 3: Cases).
2. In **ex. 3** *definiteness* is achieved by relating the property بيت to a proper noun نوري, since this refers to a specific person.
3. In **ex. 4** *definiteness* is achieved by relating the property بنك to "Mesopotamia" *(the land between the two rivers, the Tigris and the Euphrates* دجلة والفرات).

Possessive constructions may contain *more than two nouns*, as in the following examples:

the name of the manager of the company   إسمُ مديرِ الشَّركةِ

the name of the wife of the manager of the company   إسمُ زوجةِ مديرِ الشَّركةِ

*the Minister of Defence of Bahrain**   وزيرُ دفاعِ البحرين*

[Minister of Defence *property*, Bahrain *owner*]

* This example could be expressed in a different way but with the same meaning, using the adjective "Bahraini" instead of the noun "Bahrain". "Bahraini" is qualifying the *construct phrase* وزيرُ الدِّفاع:

the Bahraini Minister of Defence   وزيرُ الدِّفاعِ البحرينيّ

["Defence" is now the *owner* and takes the **definite article** as does "Bahraini"].

The examples shown above are **definite constructions**, i.e. the last element *must* be definite in order to achieve "definiteness".

However, there have to be **indefinite constructions**, i.e. *both nouns are indefinite*:

a *businessman [man of affairs]*	رجلُ أعمالٍ
a *camera [apparatus of photography]*	آلةُ تصويرٍ
a *bedroom [room of sleeping]*	غرفةُ نومٍ

An adjective may describe either part of a construct phrase:

The servant of the teacher [m] is poor	خادمُ المدرّسِ فقيرٌ
the servant of the poor teacher [m]	خادمُ المدرّسِ الفقيرِ

Notes

1. It is the proximity of the nouns next to each other, with no other word between them, that indicates a *possessive construction* (see Unit 10 for sole exceptions).
2. There is *never* a definite article «الـ» before the **property** part of the construction, i.e. the *first noun*. The **owner** word *may* or *may not* be definite (see above examples).
3. **"Definiteness"** may also be achieved by the use of *possessive pronouns* and *demonstrative pronouns*. (The use of these pronouns are covered in Units 6 and 10).
4. Any adjective qualifying an إضافة must come at the *end of the construction*.
5. For sound masculine plural and dual nouns in the construct state, see Unit 4.
6. In a construct phrase *all nouns after the first* are in the **genitive case** (see Unit 3).

Be aware that there are a number of nouns whose forms differ *from the indefinite to the definite*. Some of those which are frequently encountered in modern text include:

a *club*	نادٍ	*the club*	النَّادي
a *past*	ماضٍ	*the past*	الماضي
a *judge*	قاضٍ	*the judge*	القاضي
a *second*	ثانٍ	*the second*	الثَّاني
an *eighth*	ثمانٍ	*the eighth*	الثَّماني
a *high*	عالٍ	*the high*	العالي

These words are usually characterized by an «ı» before the final consonant in the *indefinite* and are pronounced with the ending **-in**. The *definite* words have a final *yaa'* preceded by a كسرة. In conversation, however, they are pronounced with the ending **-ii** in *both the indefinite and the definite*.

The *indefinite* of such words retains the *yaa'* in the **accusative case**, e.g. عالِياً

Note that a noun of this type retains its *yaa'* when it is the *first element of a construct phrase* because it is now considered to be definite:

the remainder of the subtraction	باقي الطَّرح
the rest of the examples	باقي الأمثلةِ

Note also that *indefinite duals* and the *feminine* are written with the *yaa'* restored. The *yaa'*, however, is **not restored** in the *sound masculine plural*:

satisfied	راضٍ	راضِيَانِ/راضِيَيْنِ	راضِيَة
	[m]	[md]	[f]

GENDER (Masculine and Feminine) المُذَكَّرُ والمُؤَنَّثُ

In Arabic, unlike English, there is no word for "it", i.e. animals and inanimate objects are classed as either **masculine or feminine** (as in French and Spanish) and both *nouns and adjectives have gender.*

A word ending with «ة» تاء مربوطة generally indicates that it is **feminine** although there are a few exceptions, e.g. *caliph* خليفة

Similarly there are many **feminine nouns** that *do not* have the feminine ending «ة»:*

earth	أرض	*desert*	صحراء
sun	شمس	*house*	دار
fire	نار	*staff*	عصا
heaven	سماء	*world*	دُنيا
well	بئر	*viper*	أفعى
*market***	سُوق	*wine***	خمر
*wind***	ريح	*war***	حرب

* Other feminine endings: ى، ا، اء
** Usually **feminine** but sometimes masculine.

These words can be either gender:

horse	فرس	*old person*	عجوز
*bride, groom**	عروس	*soul, spirit*	روح

* عريس is usually used for a *bridegroom.*

Parts of the body which occur in *pairs* are *usually* feminine:

hand	يد	*eye*	عَين
ear	أُذُن	*leg*	ساق
thigh	فخذ	*leg*	رِجْل

Exceptions

shoulder [m]	كتف	*wrist [m]*	رسغ

forearm [m]	ساعد	heel [m]	كعب
elbow [m]	مرفق	cheek [m]	خدّ

Parts of the body of which *only one* exists are *usually* **masculine**:

heart	قلب	back	ظهر
head	رأس	face	وجه
chest	صدر	throat	حلْق

Some parts of the body can be *both genders*:

breast	ثدي	arm	ذراع	foot	قَدم*

* Usually **feminine**.

Feminine words which by the nature of what they refer to are feminine:

wet-nurse	مرضع	mother	أُمّ
women	نساء	daughter	بنْت
spinster	عانس*	sister	أُخْت

* May also be used for *a bachelor* although أعزب is more commonly used.

Professions and Occupations

To create the *feminine singular* form for words denoting professions and occupations simply add «ة» to the end of the word:

	masculine	feminine
accountant	مُحاسِب	مُحاسِبة
engineer	مُهَنْدِس	مُهَنْدِسة
teacher	مُدَرِّس	مُدَرِّسة
baker	خَبّاز	خَبّازة
nurse	مُمَرِّض	مُمَرِّضة
tailor	خَيّاط	خَيّاطة
grocer	بَقّال	بَقّالة
translator	مُتَرْجِم	مُتَرْجِمة

Adjectives

Adjectives are treated in a similar way to that of professions, shown above, to create their feminine forms. An adjective following a masculine noun is masculine and an adjective following a feminine noun is feminine **and** has the feminine ending:

a wide river [m]	نهر واسع
a small car [f]	سيّارة صغيرة
a strong wind [f]	ريح شديدة

Notes

1. **Plurals of *things and abstracts*, *whether male or female*,** are regarded as **feminine singular**:

   new houses [*fs*] جديدة [*p*] بيوت

2. Names of *towns and countries* are regarded as **grammatically feminine**:

   beautiful England إنكلترا الجميلة **or**

   إنكلترا جميلة *England* [is] *beautiful**

* **Note** in Arabic the absence of a verb **"to be"** in the *present tense* (see Unit 9).

However some countries are **masculine**:

e.g. *Jordan* الأردن, *Lebanon* لبنان and *Morocco* المغرب

THE THREE CASES AND THEIR ENDINGS حَالاتُ الإِعْرَابِ

Arabic nouns, adjectives and other parts of speech have case endings which must be written and pronounced for grammatical correctness. They are always observed in readings of the Qur'an and classical literature and poetry, but are generally **ignored in speech**.

There are **three** cases in Arabic: **Nominative, Accusative and Genitive**.

Thsese cases are generally (but not always) expressed by the short vowels "u" (ضَمَّة), "a" (فتحة) and "i" (كسرة) respectively.

The short vowels which are represented by the signs (ُ ، َ ، ِ) are used for *definite* nouns and adjectives, while **nunation تَنْوِين** (ٌ ، ً ، ٍ) is used for nouns and adjectives that are *indefinite*.

Nominative الرَّفْع

The nominative is indicated by the short vowel -u ُ at the end of the word (placed above the final consonant) if the noun or adjective is *definite* (معرفة), and by the nunation -un sound) (ٌ) if the noun or adjective is *indefinite* (نكرة):

> *knowledge [is] useful* العلمُ نافعٌ

The nominative is mainly used for:

(a) the *subject* (الفاعِل) of a **verbal sentence** (جُمْلَة فِعْلِيَّة):
   The boy came جاءَ الولدُ
(b) the *subject* (المبتدأ) and *predicate* (الخبر) of a **nominal sentence** (جُمْلَة إِسميَّة):
   The doctor [is] busy الطبيبُ مشغولٌ

N.B. All nouns and adjectives should be considered to be in the *nominative case* unless otherwise indicated.

Accusative النَّصْب

The accusative is indicated by the short vowel **-a** at the end of the word if it is *definite,* and by the nunation **-an** sound (اً) if the word is *indefinite.*

The *tanwiin* is always followed by **an added** *alif,* not pronounced, *except* when the word ends with:

أ   اء*   ة   ى

* An additional أَلِف is required if the هَمْزَة is preceded by other letters:

thing شيء becomes شيئًا and *part* جزء becomes جزءًا

In modern Arabic the accusative is the **only** case ending which is indicated in print, adding a final أَلِف with *indefinite nouns and adjectives, singular and plural.*

The accusative is used for:

(a) The *object* (المفعول بِهِ) *of a* **transitive verb**:

I saw the man	شاهدتُ الرّجلَ
I saw a man	شاهدتُ رَجلاً

(b) The *indefinite* for adverbial expressions such as the English **-ly** *(quickly* سريعًا) or with phrases referring to **time** or **place**:

in the afternoon ظهرًا

Examples of adverbial expressions

The mother cares for her child day and night

تعتني الأمّ بطفلها ليلاً ونهارًا

The sun rises in the morning and sets in the evening

تشرقُ الشمسُ صباحًا وتغربُ مساءً

(c) كَمْ؟: The noun following this pronoun must be *singular and indefinite*:

How many museums have you visited? كم متحفًا زرتَ؟

(d) The *predicate of a sentence following certain* **verbs**:
(these are known as *"kaana and its sisters"* كانَ وأَخواتُها: see Unit 9)

كَانَ لَيْسَ صَارَ ظَلَّ أَمْسَى مَا زَالَ أَصْبَحَ أَضْحَى بَاتَ

*The teacher was **happy*** كانَ المعلّمُ سعيدًا

(e) The *subject* of a **nominal sentence** following one of the following **particles**:

(these are known as ***"inna and its sisters"*** إنَّ وأَخَواتُها: see unit 9)

إنَّ   أَنَّ   لَيْتَ   لَعَلَّ   كأَنَّ   لَكِنَّ   لأَنَّ

*The **house** is new* إنَّ البيتَ جديدٌ

[إنّ is an assertive particle giving a degree of emphasis and may be translated as "indeed" or omitted in translation.]

Genitive الجَرّ

The genitive case is indicated by the short vowel **-i** at the end of the word if the noun or adjective is **definite**, and by the nunation **-in** sound ( ) if the noun or adjective is **indefinite**.

The genitive is used:

(a) after prepositions:

*I'm **at** home* أنا في البيتِ

*I live **in** a house* أسكن في بيتٍ

(b) for all nouns after the first one which are part of a **construct phrase** (إضافة):

*People like **spring weather*** يحبُّ الناسُ جوَّ الربيعِ

[lit. The people like the weather of the spring]

The case of the first noun is *dependent on its function in the sentence.*

Remember! In a genitive construction the first noun *loses* its *nunation*. In the above example, although جوَّ is **indefinite** it *does not take nunation*.

The Invariable المَبْنِيّ

A word which does not change its vowel ending regardless of its grammatical function in the sentence is known as *invariable* or *indeclinable*.

Invariables include *personal pronouns, demonstrative pronouns, relative pronouns, conjunctions, most prepositions* and *interrogatives.*

Nouns which end in «ا» (e.g. عصا *rod;* باشا *pasha)* or «ى» (e.g. مرعى *meadow)* are invariable.

Foreign words which end in «ا» or «و» have **no** case ending:

إنكلترا *England* كيلو *kilo*

The Diptote غَيْرُ الْمُنْصَرِف

A number of **indefinite** words take only two case endings, the ضَمَّة (ُ) for the **nominative** and the فتحة (َ) for both the **accusative and the genitive.** A word of this type is known as a *diptote,* while a word which takes the three case endings is referred to as a *triptote* مُنْصَرِف. The *definite diptotes* behave normally and take the three case endings. **Diptotes take no nunation.**

The colours **white, black, red, green, blue** and **yellow** are diptotes (see Unit 22: The Basic Colours), and this aspect of their features is shown in the table below, using **black** as an example:

	indefinite	definite
Nominative	أسودُ	الأسودُ
Accusative	أسودَ	الأسودَ
Genitive	أسودَ	الأسودِ

Other diptotes will be pointed out as they occur.

Irregular Nouns

The following nouns, *father* أب, *brother* أخ, *father-in-law* حَم, *mouth* فُو, and *owner, possessor* ذُو are quite regular when they appear independently. However, when they act as the first element in a possessive construction **or** are joined with a pronoun suffix, then they show their case endings by means of a *long vowel,* which affects the way in which they are written **and** pronounced.

	Nominative «و»	Accusative «ا»	Genitive «ي»
your father	أَبوك	أَباك	أَبِيك
Ahmed's father	أَبو أحمد	أَبا أحمد	أَبي أحمد
your brother	أَخوك	أَخَاك	أَخِيك
Qasim's brother	أَخو قاسم	أَخا قاسم	أَخي قاسم

ذُو [ms] meaning *the owner of, possessor,* is **always the first part of a construct phrase**. In the plural it becomes ذَوُو in the **nominative**, and ذَوِي in the **accusative** and **genitive** cases. The **feminine** equivalent of ذو is ذَات [fs] and its plural is ذَوَاتُ in the *nominative* and ذَوَاتِ in the *accusative* and *genitive cases.*

Examples

Respect your [ms] father, your father-in-law and your elder brother [acc.]

إِحترَم أَبَاكَ وحماكَ وأَخَاكَ الأكبر

She took the letter from her brother's hand [gen.]

أَخَذَت الرسالةَ من يدِ أَخيها

Your [ms] brother is famous [lit. possesses fame] in Arabic literature [nom.]

أَخوكَ ذُو شهرةٍ في الأَدبِ العربي

Wash your [ms] mouth with water after the meal [acc.]

أَغسل فَاكَ بالماءِ بعدَ الطعامِ

Notes

1. In spoken Arabic case endings are generally *not pronounced* except for the **accusative** in certain dialects and for certain common words and expressions:

Thank you	شكرًا	
Thank you very much	شكرًا جزيلاً	
Don't mention it	عفوًا	
You're welcome	أهلاً وسهلاً	
very	جدًا	
comfort [said to someone who has had a bath, haircut]		نعيمًا

May you enjoy it [e.g. drink or food]   هنيئًا

2. In **adjectival clauses** that consist of a *subject and an adjective,* the adjective will have the same case ending as the subject, be that nominative, accusative or genitive:

   a long river (**nominative**)   نهرٌ طويلٌ

   I saw a fat man (**accusative**)   شاهدتُ رجلاً سمينًا

   I live in a small house (**genitive**)   أسكن في بيتٍ صغيرٍ

3. For case endings relating to duals and plurals of nouns, see Unit 4.

NOUNS AND THEIR PLURALS المُفْرَدُ والمُثَنَّى والجَمْعُ

Nouns in Arabic are either *singular, dual* (**two**) or *plural* (**three or more**) and some nouns also have a *collective plural* variation.

The **dual** form of a noun is used whenever it is preceded by the **unit 2** (as in 102, 302, 2,002 etc.) but not between 12 and 92:

202 houses   مائتَانِ وبيتَانِ

The **plural** form of a noun is used whenever it is preceded by any number **between the units 3 and 10** inclusive (as in 103, 304, 5,005 etc.) but not between 11 and 101:

304 houses   ثلاثُ مائة وأربعة بيوت

101 houses   مائةٌ وبيت

1,001 houses   ألفٌ وبيت

N.B. Nouns may have more than one plural form!

Dual المُثَنَّى

The dual is formed by the addition of a *suffix:* either «انِ» or «يْنِ» depending on the case.

Feminine			Masculine		
dual acc. and gen.	dual nom.	singular	dual acc. and gen.	dual nom.	singular
سَيِّدتَيْنِ	سيِّدتانِ	سيِّدة	رَجلَيْنِ	رجلانِ	رَجل

Note the change of the «ة» at the end of the feminine word to «ت» when a suffix is added.

The dual takes no nunation.

Note the change of the «ى» at the end of a word to «ي» when the dual suffixes are added:

a youth فَتَى becomes فَتَيَيْنِ / فَتَيَانِ

The *alif* in عصا *stick,* however, changes to *waaw* in the dual عصَوَيْنِ / عصَوانِ

There are several ways of making nouns plural in Arabic, depending on whether they are masculine or feminine, and whether they refer to people or things. They are either *sound masculine plurals, sound feminine plurals* or *broken plurals*.

Sound Masculine Plurals جَمْعُ المُذَكَّرِ السَّالِمُ

This plural is used mainly for *nouns denoting trade and profession* and for the *active participles of verbs* اسْم الفَاعِل, which *refer to people*. It is made by the addition of a *suffix:* either «ونَ» or «ينَ» depending on the case.

suffix	plural acc. and gen.	plural nom.	singular	
ونَ / ينَ	معلِّمينَ	معلِّمونَ	معلِّم	*teacher*
ونَ / ينَ	مسافرينَ	مسافرونَ	مسافر	*traveller*

Note that سَنَة *year* has the plurals سِنُونَ [nom.] and سِنِينَ [acc. and gen.] in addition to the sfp سَنَوَات. سَنَة is a contraction of سَنْوَة. The واو also appears in the plural of أُخْت, *sister,* becoming أَخَوَات.

N.B. The sound masculine plural takes no nunation.

Sound Masculine Plural and Duals in the Construct State

The «ن» endings of the *masculine plural* and *masculine and feminine duals* are omitted when these occur as the *property part* of a *construct phrase*.

the factory's engineers [mp]	مهندسو المصنع	*its engineers* [mp]	مهندسوه [mp]
to the factory's engineers [mp]	إلى مهندسِي المصنع	*to its engineers* [mp]	إلى مهندسِيه [mp]

the factory's engineers [md]	مهندسا المصنع	its engineers [md]	مهندساه
to the factory's engineers [fd]	إلى مهندستَي المصنع	to its engineers [fd]	إلى مهندستَيْه

Note these constructions:

one of the lessons of the book	درسٌ من دروسِ الكتابِ
a poem *to one of the poets*	قصيدةٌ لأحدِ الشعراءِ
research *by some scientists*	أبحاث* لِبعضِ العلماءِ

* Alternative plurals بَحْث *research* are بُحُوث، بُحُوثات

Sound Feminine Plurals جَمْعُ المُؤَنَّثِ السَّالِمُ

Most nouns that refer to females, a few masculine nouns, certain nouns that are foreign in origin and some inanimates form their plural by adding the *suffix* «ات»

acc. and gen.	nom.	plural	singular	
اتِ	اتٌ	سيّدات	سيّدة*	*lady*
اتِ	اتٌ	سيّارات	سيّارة*	*car*
اتِ	اتٌ	حيوانات	حيوان	*animal [m]*
اتِ	اتٌ	مستشفيات	مستشفى**	*hospital [m]*
اتِ	اتٌ	مؤتمرات	مؤتمر	*conference [m]*
اتِ	اتٌ	تليفزيونات	تليفزيون	*television [m]*

* The suffix «ات» is added after dropping the «ة»
** The suffix «ات» is added after changing the «ى» into «ي»

Broken Plurals جَمْعُ التَّكْسِيرِ

These plurals, also known as جَمْع مُكَسَّر, are much more complex in their structure. They are formed by breaking the word apart and arranging short and long vowels around the root letters, and in some cases adding an ending. Broken plurals, unlike sound plurals, are not limited in their use to specific areas, but are used in all situations.

The following examples are guidelines only and the final reference for the formation of a plural is to consult a dictionary.

plural	singular		notes
أَوْلاَد	وَلَد	boy	
بِلاَد	بَلَد*	country	*means country, town, community
بُلْدَان	بِلاد**		** means a specific country/ies
بُيُوت	بَيْت	house	
كِلاَب	كَلْب	dog	
عُلَب	عُلْبة	packet	
وُزَرَاء	وَزِير	minister	
كُتُب	كَتَاب	book	
أَشْهُر	شَهْر	month	
مَكَاتِب	مَكْتَب	office	
مَفَاتِيح	مِفْتاح	key	
رَسَائِل	رسالة	message	
شَوَارِع	شَارِع	street	
فَنَادِق	فُنْدُق	hotel	
أَصْدِقَاء	صَدِيق	friend	
تَلاَمِيذ / تَلاَمِذَة	تِلْمِيذ	pupil (school)	(note the plural forms)
قُمْصَان / أَقْمِصة قُمُص	قَمِيص	shirt	(note the plural forms)
دَنَانِير	دِينار	dinar	

نِسَاء/نِسْوة نِسْوَان	امْـرَأة* مَرْأة**	woman, wife	*used in the indefinite **used with the definite article
أَجْدَاد/جُدُود	جَدّ	grandfather	(note the plural forms)
آبَاء	أَب	father	
أُمَّهَات	أُمّ	mother	
إِخْوَة*/إِخْوَان**	أَخ	brother	*brothers **members of an order
أَخَوَات	أُخْت	sister	
أَبْنَاء بَنُون بَنِين	إِبْن	son	(note the plural forms) **Nominative** **Accusative and genitive**

Note that some nouns have more than one form of broken plural which have different meanings:

	plural	singular	plural	
houses	بُيُوت	بَيْت	أَبْيَات	verses
areas, regions	دِيَار	دار	دُور	houses
eminent men	أَعْيَان	عَيْن	عُيُون/أَعْيُن	eyes

Collective Nouns

Singular	Plurals	Collective Nouns	
تفّاحة	تُفّاحات	تفّاح	apple
طائِر	طُيُور	طَيْر	bird
دَجاجَة	دَجاجات	دَجاج	chicken, fowl
سَحابة	سُحُب/سَحائِب	سَحاب	cloud
بَقَرَة	بَقَرات	بَقَر	cow

نَمْرَة	تُمُور/تَمَرات	تَمْر	date (fruit)
حَمَامَة	حَمامات/حَمائِم	حَمام	dove, pigeon
زَهْرَة	زُهُور/أَزْهُر/أَزهار/ أَزاهِير/ زَهُرات	زَهْر	flower
ذُبَابَة	ذُبابات/ذِبّان	ذُباب	fly
ثَمَرَة	ثَمَرات/ثِمار/أَثْمار	ثَمَر	fruit
إِوَزَّة	إِوَزَّات	إِوَزّ	goose
لؤلؤة	لآلِئ	لؤلؤ	pearls
صَخْرة	صُخُور/صُخُورَة/صَخَرات	صَخْر	rock
وَرْدَة	وُرُود	وَرْد	rose
شَجَرَة	أَشْجار/شَجَرات	شَجَر	tree

N.B. Collective nouns of the types shown above, although plural in meaning, are usually treated as **masculine singular**:

	collective noun	plural
The dates [are] delicious	التمر لذيذ	التمور لذيذة

Notes

1. As can be seen from the above table, the collective nouns mainly apply to things in the natural world, i.e. animals, insects, plants and their fruit.
2. They are usually formed by removing the «ة», leaving the stem of the word to form the collective noun.

ADJECTIVES AND THEIR PLURALS النَّعْتُ والمَنْعُوتُ

An adjective, نَعْت or صِفَة, is a word that describes a noun. In Arabic, adjectives usually follow the nouns they describe:

a new house بيتٌ جديدٌ

Adjectives **must** agree with the nouns they qualify in **gender**, **number**, **case**, **definiteness** and **indefiniteness**:

1. *a just ruler*		حاكمٌ عادلٌ
2. *a diligent student* [f]		طالبةٌ مجتهدةٌ
3. *the old palace*		القصرُ القديمُ

In **ex.1** both the noun and the adjective are masculine singular and indefinite.

In **ex.2** both the noun and the adjective are feminine singular and indefinite.

In **ex.3** both the noun and the adjective are masculine singular and definite.

More than one adjective may follow the noun, either separated with a «و» *(and)* or not:

good, gracious manners	الأخلاقُ الكريمةُ الطيّبةُ
a marvellous and wonderful invention	اختراعٌ مدهشٌ وعجيبٌ

Plurals of Inanimates

Plurals of inanimate and abstract nouns are usually treated as **feminine** in gender regardless of the gender of the singular noun, and can be qualified by *feminine singular adjectives*, or less frequently by *plural adjectives*:

good manners	أَخلاق طيّبة
new shirts	قمصان جديدة
new shirts	قمصان جُدُد

spacious rooms	غرف واسعة
high buildings	عمارات شاهقة
high buildings	عمارات شاهقات

Feminine Plurals

Those adjectives qualifying *women* or nouns denoting *female trades and professions* follow the sound feminine plural and take the external plural ending «ات»:

lively students [fp]	طالبات نشطات
skilled cooks [fp]	طبّاخات ماهرات

When referring to a group of *mixed gender* the **masculine** adjective is used:

Dual adjective The accountant [m] and the accountant [f] [are] *busy*

المُحاسِب والمُحاسِبة مَشْغُولانِ

Plural adjective The engineers [m] and the engineers [f] [are] *absent*

المُهَنْدِسونَ والمُهَنْدِسات غائبونَ

Masculine Plurals

Sound Masculine Plural

Adjectives when used to qualify *men* or nouns denoting *male trades and professions* follow the sound masculine plural and take the external plural ending «ونَ» in the **nominative case** and «ينَ» in the **accusative** and **genitive cases**:

diligent engineers [mp] مهندسونَ مجتهدونَ

...ve internal plural forms and these are used mostly
...these are shown in the table below:

Broken Plural	
كِرام or كُرَماء	generous
سُعَداء	happy
كِبار* or كُبَراء	old (person), senior
أَغْنِيَاء	rich
أَقْوِيَاء	strong
ضِعاف or ضُعَفاء	weak
صِغَار* or صُغَراء	young

Notes

1. Some of these adjectives صِغَار* and كِبار* are also used as plural nouns, e.g. **adults** and **children**.
2. See Unit 8: Comparatives for *plurals* of **larger/est, smaller/est and greater/est**.
3. A number of adjectives, e.g. صَبُور *patient,* جَرِيح *wounded,* عَجُوز *old,* and others of similar word-shapes are used to describe **both genders**.

Adjectives in the Possessive Construction

When an adjective *precedes* a noun it qualifies it is considered to be the first part of a construct phrase and the noun *following* is **plural** in the *genitive case:*

كِبارُ الموظَّفِينَ *the important employees*

An adjective placed at the end of a construct phrase could lead to an ambiguous phrase if the adjective is written without its vowels:

سيّارةُ المعلِّمةِ الجديدة

The word جديدة *new [f],* may refer to either the first element of the construct phrase سيّارة *car* or the second element معلِّمة *teacher [f].* However, once the vowels are added the meaning becomes clear:

41

the teacher's [f] new car	سيّارةُ المعلّمةِ الجديدةُ
the new teacher's [f] car	سيّارةُ المعلّمةِ الجديدةِ

Dual Adjectives

The duals of *adjectives, masculine* and **feminine** are formed in exactly the same way as for nouns, and the patterns for the cases are also identical.

In speech, only the «يَنْ» suffix is used when qualifying dual nouns:

the **two fast** cars [f]	السيّارتَيْن السريعَتَيْن
the **two big** houses [m]	البيتَيْن الكَبيرَيْن
the **two busy** doctors [m]	الطبيبَيْن المَشْغولَيْن

In writing and formal speech, the dual adjective *must* agree with its noun in *gender* as well as *case,* i.e. the suffixes «انِ» and «يْنِ» must be used as appropriate:

In the hall [there are] **two beautiful pictures** [nom.]

في الصالةِ لوحتانِ جميلتانِ

قرأتُ قصَّتَيْنِ قصيرَتَيْنِ [acc. and gen. endings] *I read **two short stories***

Adjectives of Physical Defect

Peculiarly, the adjectives of physical defect behave in exactly the same way as *adjectives of the basic colours* (see Unit 22). To the western mind there is no logical link between these two sets of adjectives and even to the native Arabic speaker the link has been lost in the mists of time.

defect	plural *[m and f]*	feminine	masculine
deaf	طُرْش / صُمّ	طَرْشاء / صَمّاء	أَطْرَش / أَصَمّ
blind	عُمْيان / عُمْي	عَمْياء	أَعْمى
cross-eyed	زُور	زَوْراء	أَزْوَر
dumb, mute	بُكْم / خُرْس	بَكْماء / خَرْساء	أَبْكَم / أَخْرَس

flat, snub-nosed	فُطْس	فَطْساء	أَفْطَس
foolish, stupid	حُمْق / حُمُق / حَمْقى / حَماقى	حَمْقاء	أَحْمَق
foolhardy	هُوج	هَوْجاء	أَهْوَج
hunchbacked	حُدْب	حَدْباء	أَحْدَب
lame, crippled	عُرْج	عَرْجاء	أَعْرَج
one-eyed	عُور	عَوْراء	أَعْوَر

Note: Both the *singular* forms are **diptotes**.

Adjectives of Mind and Body

This is another class of adjectives that differs from the norm in the *feminine and plural*.
Note that not all adjectives ending in «ان» in the *masculine singular* behave in this way:

adjective	plural [m and f]	feminine	masculine
angry	غِضاب / غَضابى	غَضْبى	غَضْبان
drunken	سُكارى / سَكارى	سَكْرى	سَكْران
full (replete)	شَباعى / شِباع	شَبْعى	شَبْعان
hungry	جِياع	جَوْعى	جَوْعان
lazy/idle	كَسالى / كَسْلى	كَسْلة or كَسْلى	كَسْلان
thristy	عِطاش	عَطْشى	عَطْشان

Notes
1. **Both** the *singular* forms are **diptotes**.
2. The *feminine* adjectives can also be formed by adding «ة», e.g. *hungry* جوعانة.
   جائعة *hungry* is another alternative *feminine* adjective.
3. The **smp** of the *masculine* adjectives are usually used.

Diminutives التَّصْغِير

A diminutive, صِيغَةُ التَّصْغِيرِ, is often used to express endearment, contempt, ridicule, a decrease in size or number, nearness of time or place. Nouns, adjectives and some adverbs of place may form diminutives.

	diminutive		noun	
booklet	[irreg.]	كُتَيِّب	كِتاب	book
puppy		كُلَيْب	كَلْب	dog
small mountain		جُبَيْل	جَبَل	mountain
small country		دُوَيْلَة	دَوْلَة	state, country
lake [lit. small sea]		بُحَيْرة	بَحْر	sea
small star, starlet		نُجَيْمَة	نَجْم	star
time وَقْت		أُوَيْقات*	أَوْقات	times
small tree, bush		شُجَيْرة	شَجَرة	tree
a little after		بُعَيْدَ	بَعْدَ	after
a little before		قُبَيْلَ	قَبْل	before

* Plurals of diminutives usually take the *sound feminine plural ending* «ات»; however those diminutives which refer to **male humans** take the *sound masculine plural*:

little men [acc. and gen.] رُجَيْلين / [nom.] رُجَيْلُونَ ـ رُجَيْل

PERSONAL PRONOUNS

الضَّمَائِرُ المُنْفَصِلَةُ والضَّمَائِرُ المُتَّصِلَةُ

Detached Pronouns	الضمائر المنفصلة	Pronoun Suffixes	الضمائر المتَّصلة
I	أَنَا	me/my/mine	ـِي (ـنِي with verbs)
you [ms]	أَنْتَ	you/your/yours [ms]	كَ
you [fs]	أَنْتِ	you/your/yours [fs]	كِ
he	هُوَ	him/his	ـهُ
she	هِيَ	her/hers	هَا
we	نَحْنُ	us/our/ours	نَا
you [mp]	أَنْتُمْ	you/your/yours [mp]	كُمْ
you [fp]	أَنْتُنَّ	you/your/yours [fp]	كُنَّ
they [mp]	هُمْ	them/their/theirs [mp]	هُمْ
they [fp]	هُنَّ	them/their/theirs [fp]	هُنَّ
you [md and fd]	أَنْتُمَا	you/your/yours [md and fd]	كُمَا
they [md]	هُمَا	them/their/theirs [md]	هُمَا
they [fd]	هُمَا	them/their/theirs [fd]	هُمَا

Notes

1. For a mixed group of men and women, use the *masculine plural* forms.
2. The feminine plural forms are used exclusively for *female persons*. (Commonly in colloquial Arabic the *masculine plural* forms are used *instead of* the *feminine plurals*).
3. The 3rd person feminine singular form «هِيَ» is used for the *plural of things* and *abstracts*.
4. In Arabic there is only **one** pronoun suffix for the two or three used in English.
5. هُمَا، هُمْ and هُنَّ are both detached pronouns **and** pronoun suffixes.

Examples illustrating the use of *detached pronouns*:

I [am] *a teacher and you* [ms] [are] *a pupil*	أَنَا معلِّمٌ وأَنْتَ تلميذٌ
He [is] *a fine man*	هُوَ رَجلٌ لطيفٌ
She [is] *a diligent girl*	هِيَ فَتاةٌ مجتهدةٌ
We [are] *Arabs and you* [mp] [are] *English*	نَحْنُ عربٌ وأَنْتُم إِنكليزٌ

Examples illustrating the use of *pronoun suffixes* added to nouns:
These suffixes are written as part of the word they refer to and are joined directly to the last letter, unless this happens to be a non-connecting letter, in which case the suffix will stand alone, unattached:

her book	كتابٌ + ها = كتابُها
our house	دارٌ + نا = دارُنا
their [mp] *country*	بلدٌ + هُمْ = بلدُهُمْ
my wife	زوجة* + ي = زوجتِي

* **Feminine nouns** ending in «ة» change this ending to «ت» before a suffix.

The pronoun suffixes when attached to nouns convey possession and form a *possessive construction*, **nunation** is dropped and the **nouns becomes definite**:

my pen	قلمٌ + ي = قلمِي
*My school [is] *far away*	مَدْرسَتِي بعيدةٌ
Her book [is] *valuable*	كتابُها ثمينٌ
His paternal uncle [is] *a merchant*	عمُّهُ تاجرٌ
Her maternal aunt [is] *a doctor*	خالتُها طبيبةٌ

* The 1st person singular pronoun suffix ي is referred to as ياء المتكلِّم

46

Notes

1. When ي is added to a noun ending in «ا» the ي will take a -ya vowel sound:

    my stick, rod عصايَ = ي + عصا

2. The *alif* «ا» ending of the *accusative* in words like *father* أبا and *brother* أخا is omitted when the suffix of the first person singular «ي» is attached to them:

    my father and my brother أبي وأخي

3. The «ن» ending of the *dual* [m and f] and the *sound masculine plural* is dropped when suffixes are attached (see Unit 4).

Pronoun Suffixes and the Possessive Construction إِضَافَة

If the owner, المُضاف إليهِ, has two properties, المُضاف, the *second* property takes the pronoun suffix and is placed *after the owner*.

the teacher's [m] book and pencil كتابُ المدرّسِ وقلمُهُ

هُنَّ   هُمْ   هُمَا   هُ

The ضَمّة of هُ of the above suffixes changes to كسرة following a word ending in كسرة, ي or يْ ´ (see also Unit 7: Prepositions and Pronoun Suffixes):

في بيتِهِ	في بيتِهِمْ	في بيوتِهِنَّ
in his house	*in their [mp] house*	*in their [fp] houses*

Other Words which Take Pronoun Suffixes include:

بَعْض*	some	بعض + هم = بعضهم	some of them
جَميع	all	جميع + هم = جميعهم	all of them
غَيْر	other than	غير + كم = غيركم	other than you [mp]
كُلّ	all, every, each	كلّ + نا = كلّنا	all of us

لِأَنَّ	because	لِأَنَّ + ها = لِأَنَّها	because she
آخِر **	last, end	آخِر + هم = آخِرهم	last one of them
أَيّ أَيَّة	which, what	أَيّ + هما = أَيّهما أَيَّة + هما = أَيَّتهما	which one of them [md] which one of them [fd]
إِنَّ	[particle of emphasis]	إِنَّ + كَ = إِنَّكَ إِنَّ + ي = إِنِّي or إِنَّني إِنَّ + نا = إِنَّا or إِنَّنا	
كَأَنَّ	as if, though	كَأَنَّ + ها = كَأَنَّها	as if she/it
لَكِنَّ [dagger alif over the «ل»]	but, yet	لَكِنَّ + ه = لَكِنَّه	but he/it
نِصْف	fractions, e.g. half	نِصْف + ها = نِصْفها	half of her/it

* بَعْضهم بَعْضًا one another
** إلى آخِرِهِ and so forth, et cetera

إِنَّ and its sisters أَنَّ، كَأَنَّ، لَكِنَّ، لَيْتَ، لَعَلَّ take pronoun suffixes.

The word وَحْد alone is **always attached** to pronoun suffixes:
وَحْدَها she alone, on her own

Notes
1. See Unit 7 for use of the pronoun suffixes with prepositions.
2. See Unit 12 for use of the pronoun suffixes with verbs.

Unit 7

PREPOSITIONS حُرُوفُ الجَرِّ

A preposition is a word or letter placed, usually before a noun, to mark its place in either space or time. Prepositions are of two types; (a) **separate**; and (b) **attached**.

Attached prepositions: consist of only one letter and are *always connected to the word that follows*:

بِ *by, with, in*   كَ *as, like*   لِ *for, to*

Separate prepositions *[stand alone]*

فِي *in* عَنْ *from* إِلَى *to* حَتَّى *up to, as far as* مَعَ *with* عَلَى *on* مِنْ *from*

Adverbs of Place used as Prepositions

after	بَعْدَ	*with, at*	عِنْدَ	*in front of*	أَمَامَ
between	بَيْنَ	*at, by*	لَدَى	*under*	تَحْتَ
behind	وَرَاءَ	*over, above*	فَوْقَ	*around*	حَوْلَ
before [place]	قُدَّامَ	*without*	دُونَ	*against*	ضِدَّ
towards	نَحْوَ	*behind*	خَلْفَ	*before* [time]	قَبْلَ

Prepositions and Pronoun Suffixes

With the exception of كَ and حَتَّى all these prepositions take personal pronoun suffixes:

with us, in us	بِ + نَا = بِنَا
after us	بَعْدَ + نَا = بَعْدَنَا
in it/her	فِي + هَا = فِيهَا
above them [mp]	فَوْقَ + هُمْ = فَوقَهُمْ
from you [ms]	مِنْ + كَ = مِنْكَ
between him/it	بَيْنَ + هُ = بَيْنَهُ

In the above examples there are no changes in spelling or pronunciation to either the prepositions or the pronoun suffixes. However some irregularities in writing and pronunciation may occur to either the preposition or the pronoun suffix, or both, when joined together (see below).

«ي» ME
All prepositions which end in an -a vowel (فتحة) will be pronounced and written with an -i vowel (كسرة) when the first person singular pronoun suffix is added to them:

in front of me أَمامِي = ي + أَمامَ   above me فوقِي = ي + فوقَ

مِنْ from عَنْ about

from me مِنِّي = ي + مِنْ   about me عَنِّي = ي + عَنْ

In these examples the addition of «ي» doubles the «ن» using (تشديد)

فِي in

in me فِيَّ = ي + فِي

In this example «ي» of the preposition merges with the pronoun suffix and is written as a «ي» with a شدّة. The long vowel -ii sound changes to -iiya.

عَلَى on إِلَى to لَدَى at, by, with

to me إِلَيَّ = ي + إِلَى   on me عَلَيَّ = ي + عَلَى   with me لَدَيَّ = ي + لَدَى

In these examples the -a sound of the final vowel changes to -ayya, and the ى changes to يَّ in writing.

هُ HIM هُمَا هُمْ هُنَّ THEM
After prepositions ending in an -i vowel (بِ), an -ii vowel (فِي) or an -a vowel sound in words ending in «ى» like عَلَى, the هُ of the above pronoun suffixes changes from a -u vowel sound to an -i sound:

in him/it	بِهِ = هُ + بِ
in them [mp]	بِهِمْ = هُمْ + بِ
in him/it	فِيهِ = هُ + فِي
in them [mp]	فِيهِمْ = هُمْ + فِي
on them [d]	عَلَيْهِمَا = هُمَا + عَلَى

with them [mp]	لَدَى + هُمْ = لَدَيْهِمْ
to them [fp]	إلَى + هُنَّ = إلَيْهِنَّ

Note that the final -**a** vowel sound of إلَى، علَى، لَدَى changes to a diphthong -**ay** sound.

«نَا» OUR, US [suffix]

When this suffix is used with the prepositions مِنْ and عَنْ, the «ن» is doubled with a *shadda*:

from us	مِنْ + نَا = مِنَّا	*about us*	عَنْ + نَا = عَنَّا

Generally, when an unvowelled consonant is immediately followed by its twin, the two are written as a single letter with a *shadda*.

لَدَى AT, BY, WITH   إلَى TO   علَى ON

These prepositions change their ى to ي before **all** pronoun suffixes. This affects the pronunciation of the preposition and some attached pronouns (see previous example *on me* علَيَّ):

to us إلَيْنَا	*upon you [mp]* علَيْكُمْ	*with her* لَدَيْها

«لِ» TO, FOR

The كسرة in لِ changes to a فتحة before all pronoun suffixes except *me* ي:

to/for me	لِ + ي = لِي	*to/ for you [ms]*	لِ + كَ = لَكَ
to/for you [fs]	لِ + كِ = لَكِ	*to/for him [it]*	لِ + هُ = لَهُ
*to/for her [it]**	لِ + هَا = لَهَا*	*to/for us*	لِ + نَا = لَنَا

*لَها is also used with **broken plurals** and with **sfp** when *they refer to inanimates*:

هذه المدن لَها تاريخ قديم *These cities have an old history*

هذه السيّارات لَها شهرة عالميّة *These cars are well known the world over*

[lit. These cars have international fame]

This preposition *expresses possession* when joined to pronoun suffixes or nouns:

هذا الكتاب لَهُ *This book is **his***

لِلرَّجلِ بيت كبير ***The man has** a big house*

«لِ» with the Definite Article

If لِ is attached to words with the definite article then the *alif* of the article is omitted:

to the university   لِلجامعةِ = الجامعة + لِ

to the sea   لِلبحرِ = البحر + لِ

If the word starts with the letter «لِ» then the preposition merges into the word and the «لِ» of the article is also omitted:

to the colour لِلّونِ = اللّون + لِ

عِنْدَ WITH, AT

This preposition is often used as the Arabic equivalent of the verb *"to have"*:

I have	عِنْدِي = ي + عِنْدَ
You have [ms]	عِنْدَكَ = كَ + عِنْدَ
She has	عِنْدَهَا = هَا + عِنْدَ
I have three children	عِنْدِي ثلاثة أوْلاد
He has a shop	عِنْدَهُ دكّان
They [mp] have companies	عِنْدَهُمْ شركات

Notes

1. As the verb *"to have"*, عِنْدَ is used more often in spoken Arabic while «لِ» is used more frequently in writing.
2. There is a distinct difference between the use of عِنْدَ and مَعَ (both meaning *with*):

    I have no money (possess none, penniless)   ما عنْدِي فلوس

    I have no money (with me at the moment)   ما مَعِي فلوس

«كَ» LIKE, AS

This preposition *cannot take* a pronoun suffix. To make up for this, the word مِثْل is used as a substitute and means **similar, of the same kind**:

as, like me   مِثْلِي = ي + مِثْل   *like us*   مِثْلْنَا = نا + مِثْل

The noun مِثْل and the noun that follows it are in a *construct state*:

like his brother   كَأخيهِ   or   مِثْلُ أخيهِ

مِثْل is used for both masculine and feminine nouns.

«بِ» BY, WITH, IN, AT

The preposition «بِ» is always written **joined to** the noun, particle or pronoun suffix it governs:

He left by car	غادر بِالسيارةِ
The workers demanded to meet the minister	طلب العمال الإجتماع بِالوزيرِ
He came at night	حضر بِاللّيلِ
Without doubt	بِلا شكٍّ
He left hastily [lit. with haste]*	ترك بِعجلةٍ
He answered enthusiastically* [lit. with enthusiasm]	أجاب بِحماسةٍ
The servant came with the food**	جاء الخادم بِالأكلِ
Fine, thank God [lit. In well-being, praise be to God]	أنا بِخيرٍ، الحمدُ لِلّه

* In these examples, the prepositional phrase is used **adverbially**.
** Here the verb جاء, an *intransitive* verb, becomes *transitive* when followed by «بِ» and the object to which the verb refers.

Note: بَيْنَ *between:* when suffixed with a pronoun and then *followed by* a noun, بَيْنَ is repeated:

between me and the manager	بَيْني وبَيْنَ المديرِ

N.B. All *nouns that follow prepositions are in the genitive case.*

COMPARATIVES AND SUPERLATIVES صِيغَةُ التَّفْضِيلِ

Arabic uses the same words for the comparative and superlative, but they are distinguished from each other in the way they are used.

The Comparative

Sentences using the comparative form of adjectives in Arabic are constructed in much the same way as those using the comparative in English:

*Europe is **smaller than** Asia*	أوروبّا أَصْغَرُ مِن آسيا
*The elephant is **bigger than** the lion*	الفيلُ أَكْبَرُ مِن الأسدِ

The only difference is the absence of the verb **to be** *"is"* in the Arabic construction. This feature of the language has already been referred to in earlier units. The preposition مِنْ which follows the comparative is used here to express *"than"*.

Unlike adjectives, a comparative is used for *all genders* and *numbers*. The comparatives are **diptotes**.

*The house is **bigger than** the office*	البيتُ أَكْبَرُ مِن المكتب
*Fatima is **older than** Khalida*	فاطمة أَكْبَرُ مِن خالدة
*The cities are **bigger than** the villages*	المدنُ أَكْبَرُ مِن القرى

Note the use of the comparative with «ما» to express astonishment (تَعَجُّب):

*How **delicious** this food is!*	ما أَلَذَّ هذا الطعام!

A large number of comparatives are of the form أَكْبَر. A few of these and the adjectives to which they relate are listed below:

short	قَصِير	*shorter*	أَقْصَر
long, tall	طَويل	*longer, taller*	أَطْوَل
beautiful	جَميل	*more beautiful*	أَجْمَل

ugly	قَبِيح	*more ugly*	أَقْبَح
heavy	ثَقِيل	*heavier*	أَثْقَل

A few of the commonly used comparatives of this type have a *feminine* form written with a final «ى» and they may also have *separate forms for the plurals*:

*Casablanca is **one of the biggest** African cities*

الدار البيضاء مِن كُبْرِيَاتِ مدن أفريقيا

fs	mp	ms	adj	
كُبْرَى	أَكابِر	أَكْبَر	كَبِير	*big*
صُغْرَى	أَصاغِر	أَصْغَر	صَغِير	*small*
عُظْمَى	أَعاظِم	أَعْظَم	عَظِيم	*great*

Adjectives whose *second letter* is **the same as** *the fourth letter* make their comparative with this letter written with a شِدّة:

few	قَلِيل	*fewer*	أَقَلّ
intense	شَدِيد	*more intense*	أَشَدّ
new	جَدِيد	*newer*	أَجَدّ
dear	حَبِيب	*dearer*	أَحَبّ
delicious	لَذِيذ	*more delicious*	أَلَذّ
thin, gentle, delicate	رَقِيق	*thinner, more gentle, more delicate*	أَرَقّ
light	خَفِيف	*lighter*	أَخَفّ

If the second letter of an adjective is an *alif* or the third letter is «و» or «ي» the comparative is written with an «ى» at the end:

high	عالٍ	*higher*	أَعْلَى
expensive	غالٍ	*more expensive*	أَغْلَى
high-class	راقٍ	*more high-class*	أَرْقَى
sweet, pretty	خُلْوٌ	*sweeter, prettier*	أَحْلَى
clear, cloudless	صَحْو	*clearer, more cloudless*	أَصْحَى

Some adjectives, such as those which are related to **derived verbs** and **colours**, cannot form their comparatives directly. In these cases alternative constructions employing words such as أَكْثَر *more* from كَثِير *many* and أَشَدّ *stronger* from شَدِيد *strong* are used (this is the equivalent in English of *"more"* or *"most"* with longer adjectives):

more reassuring, more peaceful	أَكْثَرُ إِطمِئنَانًا
blacker	أَشَدُّ سوادًا

The Superlative

For the comparative to express the superlative it **must always be defined**:

1. He is the best doctor in the hospital*   هو أَحْسَنُ طبيبٍ في المستشفى*

2. It is the most beautiful garden in the town   هي أَجْمَلُ حديقةٍ في المدينة*

3. the smallest of villages   أَصْغَرُ القرى*

4. the prince's eldest daughter   كُبْرَى بناتِ الأمير*

5. the longest street   الشارعُ الأَطْوَلُ**

6. He is the bravest [of them]   هو أَشْجَعُهُم***

* Definiteness of the adjective is achieved by being in a *construct phrase* with its noun. The comparative is followed by an *indefinite singular noun* (ex. 1 and 2) or by a *definite plural noun* (ex. 3 and 4).
** The comparative is defined by the definite article ال. In this construction of the superlative the adjective must, as in any adjectival clause, follow its noun **and** agree with it in gender, number and definiteness.
*** Definiteness of the comparative is achieved by the *pronoun suffix*. The alternative construction هو أَكْثَرُهُم شجاعةً expresses the same meaning.

Note that in all these usages the comparative **must not** be followed by مِن in order to express the intensity of the superlative.

In the following two examples the comparative form of the adjective is used in the normal adjectival way and the superlative meaning is lost:

the great factories	المصانع العُظْمَى
Great Britain	بريطانيا العُظْمَى

THE NOMINAL SENTENCE

الجُمْلَةُ الإِسْمِيَّة: المُبْتَدَأُ والخَبَرُ

Using only the following two words together مطار *noun* and صغير *adjective* and the definite article «ال», three major fundamental Arabic constructions can be made.

Examples:

    1. **a** small airport   مطار صغير
    [an *indefinite* noun with an *indefinite* adjective]

    2. **the** small airport   المطار الصغير
    [a *definite* noun with a *definite* adjective]

    3. **The** airport **[is]** small   المطار صغير
    [a *definite* noun with an *indefinite* adjective]

Ex. 3 creates the *simplest* type of sentence in Arabic and is referred to as جُمْلَة إِسْمِيَّة. A nominal sentence consists of:
(a) a *subject* مُبْتَدَأ; and (b) a *predicate* خَبَر (what is said about the subject).

The **subject** *must be definite* and the **predicate** *indefinite*. The **verb "to be"** is absent in Arabic, but its meaning is understood in such constructions:

    the airport (subject) **(is)** *small* (predicate) المطار صغير

The **subject** is always in the *nominative case* and it can be a **noun, a proper noun** or **a personal pronoun.**

The **predicate**, an adjective, *must agree* with the subject in *gender, number* and **case.**

Examples:

    1. Knowledge [is] useful   العلمُ نافعٌ

    2. The two teachers [fd] [are] new   المعلِّمَتانِ جديدَتانِ

    3. The workers [mp] [are] satisfied   العُمَّالُ راضونَ

4. The ladies [p] [are] cultured   السيّداتُ مهذَّباتٌ

5. The houses [p] [are] new   البيوتُ جديدةٌ

Note that in each of the **ex. 1 - 4** there is an agreement between the *predicate* and the *subject* in **gender, number** and **case**.

In **ex. 5,** *"houses"* [mp] has a [fs] adjective. This is because the ***plural of inanimate nouns*** is usually treated as ***feminine in gender*** regardless of the gender of the singular noun, and takes the ***feminine singular adjective.***

Proper nouns, i.e. those that are written with a capital letter in English, are deemed to be *definite* as they refer to a specific person or place and therefore *do not* require the definite article:

Egypt [f] [is] large   مِصْرُ كبيرةٌ

Essa [is] handsome   عيسى جميلٌ

Personal pronouns are deemed to be *definite* as they also refer to a specific person, place or thing:

I [am] ill   أنا مريضٌ

It [m] [is] cold   هو باردٌ

She [is] busy   هي مشغولةٌ

In a more complicated construction **the predicate** (in brackets in the Arabic) can be a clause or a verbal sentence, as in:

The sun [is] over the earth   الشمسُ (فوقَ الأرضِ)

The palm trees [coll.] [are] in the gardens   النخلُ (في البساتينِ)

The rose, its colour [is] beautiful [lit.]   الوردةُ (لونُها جميلٌ)

The mother loves her child   الأمُّ (تُحِبُّ طفلَها)

In the garden there [are] tall trees *   (في الحديقةِ) أشجارٌ طويلةٌ

* In this example the *predicate precedes the subject* because the sentence begins with a preposition.

Kaana and its Sisters كَانَ وَأَخَوَاتُهَا

كَانَ	*was*	
صَارَ	*to become*	
أَصْبَحَ	*to wake up, to become*	
أَضْحَى	*to become*	
أَمْسَى	*to become in the evening, to be, to become*	
ظَلَّ	*to remain*	
بَاتَ	*to pass the night, to stay overnight, to spend the night*	
مَا زَالَ	*to continue to be, not to cease, is still*	
مَا دَامَ	*as long as*	
مَا بَرِحَ	*to continue to be*	
لَيْسَ	*not to be* [isn't]	

When they are used in a nominal sentence, the *predicate of these verbs* is put in the *accusative case*:

The leader was brave	كَانَ القائدُ شجاعًا
Knowledge became widespread	أَصبَحَ العلمُ سائدًا

The verb لَيْسَ, which *occurs only in the past tense* but with a *present-tense meaning*, also puts the *predicate* of a nominal sentence into the **accusative case**:

The student isn't lazy	لَيْسَ الطالبُ كسولاً

Inna and its Sisters إِنَّ وأَخَوَاتُهَا

إِنَّ	*indeed*
أَنَّ	*that*
لَعَلَّ	*perhaps, maybe*
لَكِنَّ	*but*

لَيْتَ   *if only*

لِأَنَّ   *because*

كَأَنَّ   *as if, as though*

The particle إنَّ is often used to introduce a nominal sentence for emphasis. A sentence introduced by إنَّ or one of its sisters has the **subject** in the *accusative case* and the **predicate** in the *nominative case*:

The heat [is] *intense*	إنَّ الحرَّ شديدٌ
Maybe victory [is] *near*	لَعَلَّ النصرَ قريبٌ

Note: see Unit 10 for Demonstrative Pronouns in Nominal Sentences.

DEMONSTRATIVES أَسْمَاءُ الإِشَارَةِ

The demonstratives in English are **this**, **that**, **these** and **those**.

this [m]	هَذَا	*dagger alif* over the «ه»
this [f] (**these** for plurals of **things**)	هَذِهِ	*dagger alif* over the first «ه»
that [m]	ذَلِكَ	*dagger alif* over the «ذ» no dual form
that [f] (**those** for plurals of **things**)	تِلْكَ	no dual form
these (**men and women plural**)	هَؤُلاءِ	*dagger alif* over the «ه»
those (**men and women plural**)	أُولائِكَ / أُولَئِكَ	
these [md]	*هَذَانِ *هَذَيْنِ	**nominative case** *dagger alif* over the «ه» **accusative and genitive cases**
these [fd]	*هَتَانِ / هَاتَانِ *هَتَيْنِ / هَاتَيْنِ	**nominative case** *dagger alif* over the «ه» **accusative and genitive cases**

In Arabic the demonstrative *must agree with its noun* in *gender, number and case* (duals only), and it always refers to a specific thing:

this new palace	هَذَا القصرُ الجديدُ
that old school	تِلْكَ المدرسةُ القديمةُ
that superior hotel	ذَلِكَ الفندقُ الراقي
these two diligent students *[f]*	هَتَانِ الطالبتانِ المجتهدتانِ
these many visitors *[mp]*	هَؤُلاءِ الزوّارُ الكثيرونَ

those young girls *[p]*	أُولائِكَ الفتياتُ الصغيراتُ
Those streets [are] *dirty**	تِلكَ الشوارعُ وسخةٌ*

* **Remember** that *plurals of inanimates* are regarded as feminine singular.

Notes

1. In these examples the nouns *following* demonstrative pronouns are **definite**.
2. The demonstratives have the *same* vowel endings in **all cases - invariable**.
3. The demonstratives may be *prefaced* by لِ ،كَ ،بِ e.g. بِتِلكَ = تِلكَ + بِ

Demonstratives with the Possessive Construction

Demonstratives can qualify either the *owner* المضاف إليه or the *property word* المضاف and are the *only* words that are allowed to come *between* the two elements of a possessive construction when they qualify **the owner**:

this manager's desk	مكتبُ هَذَا المديرِ
the success of **this** industry	نجاحُ هَذِهِ الصناعةِ

If the demonstrative qualifies **the property**, it will then come *after* the construction:

that gate of the palace	بابُ القصرِ ذَلِكَ
this article of yours	مقالتُكَ هَذِهِ

Demonstrative in Nominal Sentences

When the *noun that follows* the demonstrative is *indefinite* the demonstrative becomes the subject of a nominal sentence and the noun the predicate:

This [is] *a museum*	هَذَا متحفٌ
This [is] *a garden*	هَذِهِ حديقةٌ
This garden [is] *public*	هَذِهِ الحديقةُ عموميةٌ

In the last example both the demonstrative and the noun are the subject and عموميةٌ is the predicate (what is said about the subject).

When the *predicate* of the sentence is *definite* a pronoun of the third person singular, dual or plural (هُوَ، هِيَ، هُمَا، هُمْ، هُنَّ), that matches the demonstrative is inserted between the demonstrative and the predicate:

This is the clever student [ms]   هَذَا هو الطالبُ الذكيُّ

Note that when the *predicate* is defined by a pronoun suffix **or** by being a construct phrase, the use of the third person pronoun is not needed:

This [is] *my house*   هَذَا بيتي

This [is] *the student's [f] briefcase*   هَذِهِ محفظةُ الطالبةِ

Here and There هُنَا، هُنَاكَ، هُنَالِكَ

هُنَا	here
هُنَاكَ	there, over there
هُنَالِكَ	there, over there

Example:

Here in the dining room I eat the food with members of my family and there in the garden I rest with them, and over there in the school I study.

هُنَا في غرفةِ الطعامِ أَتناول الأكل مع أفراد أُسرتي وهُنَاكَ في البستان أَستريح معهم وهُنَالِكَ في المدرسة أَدرس.

Notes

1. هُنَا، هُنَاكَ and هُنَالِكَ are *invariable* **adverbs of place**.
2. As an adverb of place هُنَاكَ is used more frequently than هُنَالِكَ
3. هُنَالِكَ and هُنَاكَ are used as the *singular* and *plural* for "there is" or "there are":

   There [is] *a restaurant to the right of the hotel*

   هُنَاكَ مطعمٌ على يمين الفندق

   There [are] *many problems*   هُنَالِكَ مشاكلُ كثيرةٌ

RELATIVE PRONOUNS الأَسْمَاءُ المَوْصُولَةُ

The relative pronouns in English are *who, whom, whose, which*, and *that*.

A relative clause صلة الموصول (shown in brackets) provides additional information about its *subject*. Consider for example *"The woman whom (I met on the train)"*.

The *subject*, the woman, of the relative clause is the **antecedent** (the person or thing about which additional information is provided). The antecedent is *not necessarily* the grammatical subject of a sentence, e.g. *The police captured the man who had committed the crime*:

"*the police*" is the grammatical subject of the sentence;

"*had committed the crime*" is the relative clause;

"*the man*" is the antecedent or subject of the relative clause.

The table below lists the Arabic relative pronouns showing their gender, number and (for the duals) their cases.

ms	all cases	الَّذِي	1. male person 2. object of masculine gender
fs	all cases	الَّتِي	1. female person 2. object of feminine gender 3. plural objects of either gender
mp	all cases	الَّذِينَ	plural – male persons only
fp	all cases	اللَّاتِي اللَّوَاتِي اللَّائِي	plural – female persons only Note the extra «ل» which is *not* pronounced
dual m	nominative	اللَّذَانِ	Note the extra «ل» in all the duals which is *not* pronounced

dual m	acc. and genitive	اللَّذَيْنِ	Note the extra «ل» in all the duals which is **not** pronounced
dual f	nominative	اللَّتَانِ	Note the extra «ل» in all the duals which is **not** pronounced
dual f	acc. and genitive	اللَّتَيْنِ	Note the extra «ل» in all the duals which is **not** pronounced

Notes

1. These words are used irrespective of the English variants and are *only* used when the **antecedent is definite**.
2. Relative pronouns are *invariable*.

Examples

*1. This is the engineer **who** came to the conference*

هذا هو المهندس الَّذِي (حَضَرَ) المؤتمر

*2. This is the lady **whom** I saw in the airport*

هذه هي السيِّدة الَّتِي (رأيتُها) في المطار

*3. the lawyer from **whom** I received a letter*

المحامي الَّذِي (اسْتلمتُ مِنْهُ) كتابًا

*4. these are the two clever students [m] **who** excelled in the examination*

هذان الطالبان الذكيّان هما اللَّذَانِ (تفوَّقا) في الإمتحان

*5. the students [mp] **who** did not attend the meeting*

الطلاب الَّذِينَ لم (يحضروا) الاجتماع

*6. the cultured ladies are the ones **who** care about cultural matters*

السيِّدات المثقّفات هنَّ اللاَّتِي (يهتَمِمْنَ) بالأمور الثقافيّة

*7. the news **that** reached us two days ago was pleasing*

الأَخبار الَّتِي (وصلَتنا) قبل يومَيْن كانت مفرحة

Notes

1. In these examples the relative pronoun is used as a link between the antecedent and the relative clause.
2. The relative pronoun agrees with the antecedent in **number** and **gender** and also in **case**, but as relative pronouns are **invariable** this is observed only in the **dual** (ex. 4).
3. In Arabic there **must** be a personal pronoun in the relative clause which *agrees with* the antecedent (shown in brackets in the examples above). Such a pronoun is called *"the returning pronoun"* العائِد.

In **ex. 1, 4, 5, 6 and 7** the pronoun is *implied in the verb*.

In **ex. 2** it is *suffixed to the verb*.

In **ex. 3** it is *suffixed to a preposition* **used with the verb**.

4. In Arabic the relative clause must be able to form a complete sentence on its own.

5. In **ex. 7** the relative pronoun الَّتِي is used because the antecedent, الأَخْبار, is a plural of an inanimate.

Other pronouns used in relative sentences are:

مَنْ	*he/she/they who*	*for humans*
مَا	*what, that, which*	*for inanimates and abstracts*
أَيّ [m] أَيَّة [f]	*whichever, whoever*	

Examples:

*He **who** steals shall be punished*   مَنْ يسرقْ يُعاقَبْ

*I was surprised by **what** I saw in the square*
[lit. It surprised me]   أدهشني مَا رأيتُ في الميدان

*We will go to **whichever** restaurant you prefer*
نذهب إلى أَيّ مطعمٍ تُفَضِّل

Relative Sentences with Indefinite Antecedents

If the antecedent is **indefinite** the relative pronoun is *omitted* and the relative clause is called نعت or صفة:

*The teacher reprimanded **a pupil** who came late*
وَبَّخَ المعلِّمُ تلميذًا حَضَرَ متأخرًا

*Granada is **a city** in which there are many gardens*
غرناطة مدينة فيها حدائقُ كثيرة

The *returning pronoun* is *implied in the verb* حَضَرَ in the first example and *suffixed to the preposition* في in the second example.

N.B. The rule is that *no* relative pronouns are used with indefinite antecedents!

THE PAST TENSE الفِعْلُ المَاضِي

Introduction to the Arabic Verb

The verb in Arabic differs from that in English in these respects:
1. It has a masculine and a feminine form.
2. It has a dual form for the 2nd and 3rd persons.
3. It has a plural form for the 1st, 2nd and 3rd persons.
4. There is no equivalent in Arabic of the *infinitive form* of the verb in English:

   I want to study [lit. I want I study] أريدُ أدرسُ
5. Generally it is not necessary to use personal pronouns with verbs because the suffixes (together with the prefixes in the case of the present tense) act as a substitute for these and convey the same information.

The Past Tense

The past tense, also referred to as the **Perfect**, denotes a completed action. In Arabic the simplest form of the verb is the **past tense of the 3rd person masculine singular**, i.e. the **he-form**. This is because it has no written prefixes or suffixes. The verb mostly consists of three consonants (فِعْل ثُلاَثِيّ), although there are some which consist of four consonants (فِعْل رُبَاعِيّ):

   بَرْهَنَ *he proved* تَرْجَمَ *he translated*

The **3rd person singular** is of three patterns, of which the *first* and *third consonants* all have فتحة:

   Pattern 1: the middle consonant has فتحة كسرة e.g. كَتَبَ *he wrote*

   Pattern 2: the middle consonant has كسرة e.g. شَرِبَ *he drank*

   Pattern 3: the middle consonant has ضمّة e.g. كَثُرَ *to be numerous*

The stem of the past tense *for any verb* is obtained by dropping the last vowel of the *he-form* past tense of the verb. Conjugation of the verb is achieved by adding suffixes to the stem. These suffixes perform the function of the subject (subject markers). The vowels on the first and second consonants are retained as in its stem throughout the conjugated forms. Conjugation of the verb كَتَبَ *he wrote,* as an example of Pattern 1, is shown in the table below.

Verbs belonging to Patterns 2 and 3 are conjugated in the past tense in a similar way as those of Pattern 1.

	suffixes	*he WROTE* كَتَبَ
I wrote	...ْتُ	كَتَبْتُ
you wrote [ms]	...ْتَ	كَتَبْتَ
you wrote [fs]	...ْتِ	كَتَبْتِ
he wrote	...	كَتَبَ
she wrote	...َتْ	كَتَبَتْ
we wrote	...ْنَا	كَتَبْنَا
you wrote [mp]	...ْتُمْ	كَتَبْتُمْ
they wrote [mp]	...ُوا	كَتَبُوا
you wrote [fp]	...ْتُنَّ	كَتَبْتُنَّ
they wrote [fp]	...ْنَ	كَتَبْنَ
you wrote [md]	...ْتُمَا	كَتَبْتُمَا
you wrote [fd]	...ْتُمَا	كَتَبْتُمَا
they wrote [md]	...َا	كَتَبَا
they wrote [fd]	...َتَا	كَتَبَتَا

Notes

1. In colloquial Arabic the short vowels at the end of the past tense for: **I, you (ms), you (fs)** and **he** are generally not pronounced.

2. نا is a verb suffix as well as pronoun suffix *(us, our, ours)* (see Unit 6).

3. These rules for conjugating the past tense apply to all **sound verbs (فعل سالم)**, i.e. verbs which are devoid of the weak letters «و» or «ي» (the weak letters, **حروف العلّة**, are «ا» «و» and «ي»), or verbs which have their second and third radicals identical *(double verbs)*, or verbs in which one radical is a *hamza (hamzated verbs)*.

Some minor changes are made when ***non-sound verbs*** are conjugated (see Unit 17).

4. Verbs ending with «ن» when they take the subject marker «نَا» or «نَ» are written with a single «ن» with a *shadda:*

    we declared أعلنَّا   *he declared* أعلنَ

Similarly, verbs ending with «ت» when they are suffixed by, تُمَا، تُنَّ، تُمْ، تِ، تَ، تُ are written with a single «ت» with a *shadda.*

Word Order and Verb Subject Agreement

In general the **verb** الفعل comes *first* followed by the **subject** الفاعل, which is the *"doer"* of the action expressed by the verb. However the subject may precede the verb for reasons of style or emphasis.

A sentence that begins with a verb is referred to as a *verbal sentence* جملة فعليّة.

If the verb is **transitive** فعلٌ متعدٍّ it will take an object المفعول به, which usually comes *after the subject*. Frequently the sentence has more than one verb related to the same subject (see **ex. 3, 8 and 9** below), and these follow the subject and the object, if any, and **must** agree with the subject in *gender and number*. However, if the subject is a plural of an inanimate or abstract, the verb is 3rd person feminine singular.

The verb when it *precedes* its subject is **always 3rd person singular** irrespective of whether the subject is singular, dual or plural. In this instance the verb agrees with its subject in *gender only*.

However, the 3rd person feminine singular verb is used when the subject is a broken plural referring to inanimate objects or abstracts. With some broken plurals a feminine **or** masculine verb may be used.

Examples

1. *We have studied and played*   دَرَسْنَا ولَعِبْنَا

2. *The ambassador [m] arrived*   وَصَلَ السفيرُ

3. *The student wrote the letter and sent it*   كَتَبَ الطالبُ الرسالةَ وأَرْسَلَهَا

4. *The two merchants [m] travelled*   سَافَرَ التاجرانِ

5. *The teachers [mp] and the pupils [mp] have returned*

عَادَ المعلِّمونَ والتلاميذُ

6. *The girl put on her raincoat*

لَبِسَتِ الفتاةُ معطفَها

7. *The teachers [fd] visited the museum*

زَارَتِ المعلِّمتانِ المتحفَ

8. *The teachers [fp] and students [fp] travelled to Riyadh then returned to Dubai*

سَافَرَتِ المدرِّساتُ والطالباتُ إلى الرياض ثم رَجَعْنَ إلى دبي

9. *The members of the family ate and drank*

أَكَلَ أفرادُ الأسرةِ وشَرِبُوا

10. *Four teachers [fp] joined the school this year*

إِلْتَحَقَ بالمدرسةِ هذا العامَ أربعُ مدرِّساتٍ

11. *The remaining ancient monuments indicated...*

دَلَّتِ الآثارُ الباقيةُ...

12. *The distrubances which took place in the district*

الإضطراباتُ التي وَقَعَتْ في المنطقةِ

13. *The newspapers published this resolution* قَدْ نَشَرَتِ الصحفُ هذا القرارَ

ex. 1	In this example the *pronoun* is omitted because it is understood from the subject marker (نَا). The *pronoun* is **only** written when emphasis is required.
ex. 2	The *verb* is **3rd person masculine singular** and the *subject* is **masculine singular**. The subject is in the **nominative case** as shown by the ضمّة on the final consonant.
ex. 3	الطالبُ *the student* is the subject and is in the **nominative case** as shown by the ضمّة on the final consonant. الرسالةَ *the letter* is the object of the verb and is in the **accusative case** as shown by the final فتحة
ex. 4 and 5	The verbs are **3rd person masculine singular** and the subjects are **masculine dual** and **plural** respectively.
ex. 6 and 7	The verbs are **3rd person feminine singular** and the subjects are **singular** and **dual feminine** respectively.
ex. 8	The verb سَافَرَتِ is **3rd person feminine singular** and the subject is **sound feminine plural**. The second verb رَجَعْنَ is feminine plural in agreement with the subject **[fp]** because the **subject precedes the verb.**
ex. 6, 7 and 8	The ـتْ at the end of each verb is changed into ـتِ because the verbs are followed by words beginning with two consonants. This is done for phonetic reasons.

ex. 9   The verb شَرِبُوا and the subject أفرادُ الأسرةِ are both *masculine plural* and are in agreement because the *subject precedes the verb.*

The final «ا» in verbs ending in «وا» is **not pronounced**.

ex. 10   The verb إِلْتَحَقَ is *3rd person masculine singular* and the subject, أربعُ مدرِّساتٍ, is *feminine plural*. This is because the subject is separated from the verb by intervening words. In such situations **either** a masculine **or** feminine verb could be used.

The verb إِلْتَحَقَ is a *derived* verb (المزيد). It is formed from the basic stem لَحَقَ (see Unit 18: Derived Forms of the Verb).

ex. 11 and 12 The verbs are *3rd person feminine singular* because the subjects are *plurals of inanimates.*

ex. 13   The particles قَدْ and لَقَدْ, when they occur *before the past tense*, emphasize the completion of the action and may be translated as *indeed, really* or *already,* or they may be omitted in translation.

Verbs with Pronoun Suffixes

In Units 6 and 7 we saw how the pronoun suffixes can be attached to nouns and prepositions respectively. In much the same way these suffixes can be added to verbs to express their objects.

Note that the pronoun suffix corresponding to the *1st person singular* when attached to verbs is different from that used with nouns and prepositions. It is «نِي» when attached to verbs and «يِ» with nouns and prepositions:

He asked me	سَأَلَنِي = نِي + سَأَلَ
my house	بيتِي = ي + بيت
in front of me	أمامِي = ي + أمام

Note how vowelling distinguishes between the different meaning of verbs ending with نَا:

We informed	أَخْبَرْنَا
He informed us	أَخْبَرَنَا

The first example consists of the verb with its subject marker.

The second example consists of the verb and the pronoun suffix نَا.
In an unvowelled text the meaning of each word will be understood from the context.

The following notes need to observed when *pronoun suffixes are added to verbs:*

1. The final *alif* in verbs ending in «وا» is dropped:

    They [mp] wrote it [f]   كَتَبُوا + هَا = كَتَبُوهَا

    They [mp] took us   أَخَذُوا + نَا = أَخَذُونَا

2. For *2nd person masculine plural* verbs ending in «تُمْ», a «و'» is added before the pronoun suffix:

    You [mp] sent it [f]   أَرْسَلْتُمْ + هَا = أَرْسَلْتُمُوهَا

3. Verbs which end with «ى» change it to «ا» (ألف قائمة) when a pronoun suffix is added to them:

    He delivered it [f]   أَلْقَى + هَا = أَلْقَاهَا

    He cancelled it, nullified it [m]   أَلْغَى + هُ = أَلْغَاهُ

4. Pronoun suffixes, because they express the object of the verb, are sometimes referred to as *"object suffixes"*.

Negation of the Past Tense

To negate the past tense the particle مَا is placed before the verb:

The train arrived   وَصَلَ القطارُ

*The train **did not** arrive*   مَا وَصَلَ القطارُ

Negation and **Prohibition** are discussed fully in Unit 24.

THE PRESENT TENSE الفِعْلُ المُضَارِعُ

The present tense in Arabic is used for actions that are not yet complete and is equivalent to the *present tense* or the *present continuous tense* in English.

The present tense is formed according to a regular and easily applied set of rules. Each verb consists of a stem, which denotes the action of the verb, to which are added prefixes and sometimes also suffixes to indicate the different persons. These prefixes and suffixes are constant from one verb to another, be it a simple verb or a derived form. The vowelling of the prefixes, however, are different for some of the derived forms.

The following points apply to *sound verbs*:

1. The stem of the *present tense* mostly consists of *three consonants*. These consonants are the same as those of the stem of the *past tense* but they differ in their vowels.

2. The **first consonant** of the stem has a *sukuun,* i.e. it has no vowel. This is true for verbs of **Forms I, IV, VII, VIII, IX** and **X**. This is not the case with quadriliteral verbs. For **Forms II, III, V, VI** and *quadriliteral verbs* the first consonant of the stem takes a فتحة.

3. The **second consonant** of the stem can have any of the short vowels, فتحة, كسرة or ضمّة, and this vowel *remains unchanged* for all the different persons. This vowel is best learned together with its root verb, otherwise it must be ascertained from the dictionary.

4. The **third consonant** of the stem, for those verbs that do not have a suffix, ends in a ضمّة vowel.

Examples

He goes to school by bicycle	يَذْهَبُ إلى المدرسة بالدرّاجة
The teacher [m] speaks and the pupils listen	
المعلِّم يَتَكَلَّمُ والتلاميذُ يُنْصِتُونَ	
Khalida studies at Cairo University	خالدة تَدْرُسُ في جامعة القاهرة
We buy woollen clothes in the winter [lit. in the season of winter]	
نَشْتَرِي الثيابَ الصوفيّةَ في فصلِ الشتاءِ	

Parents [d] help [one another] *in the upbringing of their [d] children*

الوالدان يَتَعَاوَنَانِ في تربيةِ أولادِهما

The nurses [fp] attend to the comfort of the patients

الممرِّضات يَسْهَرْنَ على راحة المرضى

The conjugation of the present tense verb يَكْتُبُ *he writes* is set out in the table below:

Detached Pronouns	الضمائر المنفصلة	Additions to the verb stem	The Verb الفعل *Indicative*
I	أَنَا	أَ...‎	أَكْتُبُ
you [ms]	أَنْتَ	تَ...‎	تَكْتُبُ
you [fs]	أَنْتِ	تَ...ِينَ	تَكْتُبِينَ
he	هُوَ	يَ...‎	يَكْتُبُ
she	هِيَ	تَ...‎	تَكْتُبُ
we	نَحْنُ	نَ...‎	نَكْتُبُ
you [mp]	أَنْتُمْ	تَ...ُونَ	تَكْتُبُونَ
they [mp]	هُمْ	يَ...ُونَ	يَكْتُبُونَ
you [fp]	أَنْتُنَّ	تَ...ْنَ	تَكْتُبْنَ
they [fp]	هُنَّ	يَ...ْنَ	يَكْتُبْنَ
you [md]	أَنْتُمَا	تَ...َانِ	تَكْتُبَانِ
you [fd]	أَنْتُمَا	تَ...َانِ	تَكْتُبَانِ
they [md]	هُمَا	يَ...َانِ	يَكْتُبَانِ
they [fd]	هُمَا	تَ...َانِ	تَكْتُبَانِ

The present tense stem of this verb is: كْتُبُ

For verbs of **Forms II, III, IV** and **Form I** of quadriliteral verbs, the present tense prefixes are vowelled "**u**" instead of "**a**":

    Form II   *I manage*   أُدَبِّرُ

Form III	he travels	يُسَافِرُ
Form IV	she does well	تُحْسِنُ
Quadriliteral	he translates	يُتَرْجِمُ

Verbs ending with «ن» when suffixed by «نَ» (**you** *[fp]* and **they** *[fp]*) are written with a single «ن» with a *shadda*.

Moods of the Present Tense

The *present tense* has three moods:

1. **Indicative** المضارع المرفوع   (This refers to the ordinary form of the *present*).

2. **Jussive** المضارع المجزوم
3. **Subjunctive** المضارع المنصوب

The Jussive Mood المضارع المجزوم

The negating particle لَمْ when used with a *present tense* verb gives the meaning of the **negated past**, although its grammatical tense has not changed:

| *We **did not go** with them [mp]* | لَمْ نَذْهَبْ معهم |
| *We **did not go** with them [mp]* | مَا ذَهَبْنَا معهم |

The verb نَذْهَبْ, in the first of the two sentences above, is without a final vowel and is said to be in the *jussive mood*. All verbs which end with ضمّة in the *indicative mood* lose their terminal vowel in the *jussive*. Some parts of the verb which end with «ن» in the *indicative mood* lose this when in the *jussive*. Thus *"to write"* كَتَبَ becomes:

You [fs]	تكتبين	preceded by لَمْ becomes	تكتبي
You [md and fd]	تكتبان	preceded by لَمْ becomes	تكتبا
You [mp]	تكتبون	preceded by لَمْ becomes	تكتبوا
They [md]	يكتبان	preceded by لَمْ becomes	يكتبا
They [fd]	تكتبان	preceded by لَمْ becomes	تكتبا
They [mp]	يكتبون	preceded by لَمْ becomes	يكتبوا

Notes

1. The final «ن» of the 2nd person feminine plural and the 3rd person feminine plural is *retained* in the *jussive*.
2. An *alif* is written after the *waaw* of the 2nd and 3rd person masculine plural. This *alif* is not pronounced.
3. The *jussive* is also used in the following situations:
   (a) with the *negative imperative* «لا» (لا النَّاهِية):
       Don't write on the book لا تَكْتُبْ على الكتاب
   (b) after the «ل» of the *imperative* (لام الأمر):
       Let each one of us do his work لِيَقُمْ كلٌّ مِنّا بعمله
   (c) in conditional sentences (see Unit 28).

Jussive of Hollow Verbs

A hollow verb is one which has one of the weak letters **before** the last consonant.

In the *jussive* of such verbs the *long vowel* of the *indicative* is replaced by the corresponding *short vowel*:

1. He was not in the house	لم يَكُنْ في البيت
2. She was unable to help him	لم تَسْتَطِعْ مساعدته

This shortening **does not occur** when the verb has an attached suffix:

لم يستطيعُوا *they [mp] were not able* يستطيعُون *they [mp] can*

In **ex. 1**, يَكُنْ is 3rd person masculine singular *jussive* and corresponds to the *indicative* يَكُونُ

In **ex. 2**, تَسْتَطِعْ is 3rd person feminine singular *Form X jussive* and corresponds to the *indicative* تَسْتَطِيعُ

Weak verbs ending with «ى» ،«ي» or «و» (فعل ناقص) drop these letters in the *jussive* and are replaced by the corresponding short vowels:

he remains	يَبْقَى	*he did not remain*	لم يَبْقَ
he comes	يَأْتِي	*he did not come*	لم يَأْتِ
he invites	يَدْعُو	*he did not invite*	لم يَدْعُ

The Subjunctive Mood المضارع المنصوب

The *subjunctive* of the *present tense* is used after the following conjunctions:

that	أَنْ	(أَلَّا = لا + أَنْ) *that not*	أَلَّا
so that	لِ...	(لِئَلَّا = لا + لِأَنْ) *lest*	لِئَلَّا
so that	لِأَنْ	*will not, will never*	لَنْ
so that	كَيْ	*so that* (فاء السببيّة)	فَ
so that	لِكَيْ	*so that* (واو المعيّة)	وَ
so that	حَتَّى		

The *subjunctive* form is used to express a wish or purpose:

1. *He asked me to write the report*   طَلَبَ مني أَنْ أَكْتُبَ التقريرَ

2. *The farmer gets ready to plough the land*

يَسْتَعِدُّ الفلاحُ لِيَحْرُثَ الأرض

3. *We must respect the rules of conduct*   عَلَيْنَا أَنْ نَحْتَرِمَ آدابَ السلوك

Notes

In **ex. 1**, the verb أَكْتُبَ is 3rd person masculine singular *subjunctive*. The sign of the subjunctive is a final فتحة.

In **ex. 2**, the verb يَسْتَعِدُّ is 3rd person masculine singular **Form X** of the doubled verb عَدَّ *to count*. يَحْرُثَ is 3rd person masculine singular *subjunctive*.

In the *singular* the sign of the *subjunctive* is a final فتحة for all persons except the 2nd person feminine, and in the *plural* the 1st person plural also has a final فتحة. In otherwords all parts of the verb which end with ضمّة in the *indicative mood* end with فتحة in the *subjunctive mood*.

Those parts of the verb which lose their «ن» in the *jussive* also lose it in the *subjunctive*.

Present Tense with Pronoun Suffixes

Pronoun suffixes when added to the present tense express the *object* of the verb just as they do when added to the past tense:

He puts it [f]   يَضَعُ + هَا = يَضَعُهَا

He takes them [mp]	يَأْخُذُ + هُمْ = يَأْخُذُهُمْ
You [mp] find him	تَجِدُونَ + هُ = تَجِدُونَهُ

Note that the «ى» at the end of verbs changes to «ا» when a pronoun suffix is added:

أَرَى	أَرَاهُ	أَرَاهَا
I see	*I see him*	*I see her*

Verb Subject Agreement

The rules for the agreement of the subject and the past tense verb were discussed in the previous unit. These rules equally apply to the *present* and *future tenses*.

The Future Tense المُسْتَقْبَلُ

The future can be expressed in a number of ways:

1. By placing the word سَوْفَ immediately *before* the verb in the *present tense:*

    سَوْفَ أَكْتُبُ التقريرَ الأسبوعَ القادمَ *I'll write the report next week*

    Note that سَوْفَ **is invariable.**

2. By attaching the letter «سَ» (a shortened form of سَوْفَ) to the verb in the *present tense:*

    سَأَرُوحُ يومَ السبتِ *I will go on Saturday*

3. The future tense can also be expressed by the use of the *simple present tense* with future time phrases, e.g. **tomorrow, after, next**, etc.

    أَرْجِعُ بعدَ نصفِ ساعةٍ *I will return in (after) half an hour*

    أَعُودُ الأسبوعَ القادمَ *I will come back next week*

See **Unit 16:** كَانَ *kaana* for additional notes on the formation of the future tense.

THE IMPERATIVE فِعْلُ الأَمْرِ

The imperative is used for issuing orders or giving instructions.

The form the imperative takes depends on whether it is used to address a man, a woman, two people, a group of men or a group of women. For a mixed group, use the masculine plural form.

Formation of the Imperative

The imperative, with few exceptions, is formed according to the following rules:

1. It is formed from the **2nd person jussive singular, dual** and **plural** by removing the prefix. If the resulting form begins with a consonant followed by a vowel, this becomes the imperative:

	Jussive	**Imperative**	
you [ms] Form I	تَقُلْ	قُلْ	*say!*
you [ms] Form I	تَقِفْ	قِفْ	*stop!*
you [ms] Form II	تُصَرِّحْ	صَرِّحْ	*declare!*
you [fs] Form III	تُسافِرِي	سَافِرِي	*travel!*
you [ms] Quadriliteral	تُتَرْجِمْ	تَرْجِمْ	*translate!*
you [mp] Form V	تَتَعَلَّمُوا	تَعَلَّمُوا	*learn!*
you [fs] Form VI	تَتَبَادَلِي	تَبَادَلِي	*exchange!*

2. If after removing the prefix from the *jussive,* as described above, the resulting form begins with a vowelless consonant, the prefix is replaced by a هَمْزة (carried on an *alif*) with a helping vowel. The vowel applied to the هَمْزة is ضَمّة if the vowel of the second radical of the jussive is ضَمّة. Otherwise it is a كسرة:

	Jussive	form of «ء»	Imperative	
you [ms]	تَكْتُبْ	أ	أُكْتُبْ	write!
you [ms]	تَشْرَبْ	إ	إشْرَبْ	drink!
you [ms]	تَجْلِسْ	إ	إجْلِسْ	sit!
you [fs]	تَكْتُبِي	أ	أُكْتُبِي	write!
you [md and fd]	تَكْتُبَا	أ	أُكْتُبَا	write!
you [mp]	تَكْتُبُوا	أ	أُكْتُبُوا	write!
you [fp]	تَكْتُبْنَ	أ	أُكْتُبْنَ	write!
you [ms] Form X	تَسْتَأْنِفْ	إ	إسْتَأْنِفْ	appeal!

Note that **Form IV** verbs always take أ in the formation of their imperatives:

	Jussive	Imperative	
you [ms]	تُحْسِنْ	أَحْسِنْ	do well!
you [ms]	تُخْبِرْ	أَخْبِرْ	notify!
you [ms]	تُرْسِلْ	أَرْسِلْ	send!

An alternative method for forming the imperative of **Forms II, III, IV, VII, VIII, IX*** and **X** from *sound past tense verbs* is by omitting their suffix and changing the فتحة vowel of their penultimate radical into a كسرة vowel:
* Form IX is quite rare and is used only to denote the action of **acquiring primary colours** or **becoming bodily defective**.

	Past Tense	Imperative	
you [ms] Form II	عَلَّمْتَ	عَلِّمْ	teach!
you [ms] Form III	كَاتَبْتَ	كَاتِبْ	correspond!
you [ms] Form IV	أَجْلَسْتَ	أَجْلِسْ	be seated!
you [ms] Form VII	إنْكَسَرْتَ	إنْكَسِرْ	be broken!
you [ms] Form VIII	إجْتَمَعْتَ	إجْتَمِعْ	assemble!
you [ms] Form X	إسْتَعْمَلْتَ	إسْتَعْمِلْ	use!

For **Forms V** and **VI** the method is similar to that outlined above but the vowel of the penultimate radical, after omitting the subject marker, is retained as فتحة:

	Past Tense	Imperative	
you [ms] **Form V**	تَعَلَّمْتَ	تَعَلَّمْ	*learn!*
you [ms] **Form VI**	تَبَادَلْتَ	تَبَادَلْ	*exchange!*

The *feminine singular, dual [m and f], masculine plural* and *feminine plural forms* are formed by adding the suffixes ي، ا، وا، نَ respectively, e.g. the imperative تَعَلَّمْ *learn! [ms]* becomes:

learn! [fs]	تَعَلَّمِي	*learn!* [m and f dual]	تَعَلَّمَا
learn! [mp]	تَعَلَّمُوا	*learn! [fp]*	تَعَلَّمْنَ

Note the change of the سكون on the final consonant into a كسرة to accompany the ي, into فتحة to accompany the «ا», and into ضمّة to accompany the وا.

Finally there are a few imperatives **not formed** from their verbs as described by the above methods:

	Jussive	Imperative	
you [ms]	تَأْكُلْ	كُلْ	*eat!*
you [ms]	تَأْخُذْ	خُذْ	*take!*
you [ms]	تُؤَدِّ	أَدِّ	*convey!*

The imperatives تَعَالَ *come!* and هاتِ *give! bring me!* exist **only** in their *imperative forms*.

Negative Commands

Negative commands are formed by putting «لا» (لاَ النَّاهِيَة) before the *2nd person jussive* according to the person(s) addressed:

don't say	[to a woman]	لا تَقُولِي

don't go	[to men]	لا تَذْهَبُوا
don't write	[to a man]	لا تَكْتُبْ

The Verb يَجِبُ "it is necessary" or "must"

The 3rd person masculine singular verb is always used regardless of what is being talked about. It is followed by أَنْ and the *present tense* or by a *verbal noun* without the use of أَنْ:

it is necessary that you [ms], you [fs], he, we . . .

يَجِبُ عليكَ/ عليكِ/ عليهِ/ علينا... أَنْ

It is necessary to construct new factories   يَجِبُ إنشاءُ مصانع جديدة

"**should have**" is expressed by placing كـان in front of the above constructions:

We should have attended the meeting

كان يَجِبُ علينا أن نحضرَ الإجتماع

The *past tense* وَجَبَ is used similarly:

He had to travel   وَجَبَ عليهِ السفرُ

"**have to**" may also be expressed by على followed by its object, أَنْ and the *present tense* or by the *verbal noun* without the use of أَنْ:

You have to be cautious   عليكَ أَنْ تكونَ حذرًا

Below is a short passage with its translation illustrating the use of the imperative:

هذه نصائحُ جَدّ لأحفاده:

إسمعوا يا أبنائي، فخذوا نصائحي واعملوا بها.

كونوا مؤدَّبين في معاملاتكم.

احترموا من هم أكبر منكم سِنًّا.

اعتمدوا على أنفسكم.

أدّوا واجباتكم واعملوا دائمًا بجِدّ وإخلاص.

ساعدوا أصدقاءكم إذا طلبوا منكم.

ناصروا الضعفاءَ وعاملوهم بالرِّفقِ، ودافعوا عن حقوق المظلومين.

أوفوا بالعهد.

ادعوا إلى الخير وانهوا عن الشرّ.

This is [these are] a grandfather's advice [advices] to his grandchildren:
Listen, my children, take my advice [advices] and act upon it [them].
Be polite in your conduct [conducts].
Respect those who are older than you [in age].
Depend upon yourselves.
Carry out your obligations and always work with diligence and sincerity.
Help your friends if they ask you.
Support the weak and treat them with kindness and defend the rights of the unjustly treated.
Fulfil your commitments.
Call for good and ban evil.

[Literal translation in square brackets.]

THE PASSIVE الفِعْلُ المَبْنِيُّ لِلمَجْهُولِ

The use of the passive verb in Arabic is somewhat different from that in English. In Arabic it is only used when the *agent* is unknown, and for this reason it is called المجهول, *"the unknown":*

> *The door was opened* فُتِحَ البابُ

The person or thing *(the agent)* who carried out the action (the *"opening"* in the above example) is not mentioned.

The noun that comes *after* the passive verb, نائب الفاعل, is in the **nominative case.**

Note that both the active (المعلوم) and passive verbs, in the majority of cases, differ only in their vowelling, and would therefore look identical in unvowelled texts. However the context will make clear whether a passive or active verb is intended.

Formation of the Passive

The Past Tense

The passive past tense of *sound verbs* is formed from the **root** of the corresponding verb by making the vowel of the first consonant ضمّة (ُ) and that of the penultimate consonant كسرة (ِ). The *verb endings* are unaffected.

The passive is conjugated in exactly the same manner as the active:

	Active Past Tense	**Passive Past Tense**	
he wrote	كَتَبَ	كُتِبَ	*it was written*
she wrote	كَتَبَتْ	كُتِبَتْ	*it was written*
they [mp] killed	قَتَلُوا	قُتِلُوا	*they were killed*
he translated	تَرْجَمَ	تُرْجِمَ	*it was translated*

84

This method for forming the passive past tense also applies to verbs **Forms II** and **IV**:

he granted	خَوَّلَ	II	خُوِّلَ	it was granted
he managed	دَبَّرَ	II	دُبِّرَ	it was managed
he declared	أَعْلَنَ	IV	أُعْلِنَ	it was declared

If the verb ends with an **ألف** (ا or ى) in the *past tense*, this is changed into يَ and a **ضمّة** and a **كسرة** are applied to the first and the penultimate consonants respectively:

	Active Past Tense	**Passive Past Tense**	
he arrested	أَلْقَى	أُلْقِيَ	he was arrested
he invited	دَعَا	دُعِيَ	he was invited
he related	رَوَى	رُوِيَ	it was related

The Present Tense

The passive present tense of *sound verbs* is formed from the corresponding active by giving a **ضمّة** to the prefix (subject marker) and a **فتحة** to the penultimate consonant. The verb endings are unaffected:

	Active Present Tense	**Passive Present Tense**	
he opens	يَفْتَحُ	يُفْتَحُ	it will be opened/ is opened
he strikes	يَضْرِبُ	يُضْرَبُ	he will be struck/ is struck

This rule also applies to the *derived verbs*. However, some of these have a passive meaning, particularly **Forms VII** and **VIII**. **Form IX** does not have a passive.

Again the *present passive* is conjugated in the same manner as the *active:*

يُتْرَكُ	تُتْرَكُ	نُتْرَكُ
he is left	she is left	we are left

N.B. The formation of the passive of *hollow verbs* and some *hamzated verbs* does not follow the rules outlined above. These verbs can be studied in Raymond Scheindlin, *201 Arabic Verbs,* (Barron's Educational Series, New York, 1978).

THE VERB كَانَ

The verb كَانَ or its *present tense* form يَكُون has **two** distinctly different uses depending on whether it is used as the only verb in the sentence, or is used in combination with a second verb.

1. When كَانَ is used as the **only** verb in the sentence it is translated into English as *"was"*, while the present tense, يَكُون, is translated as *"will be"*:

The cold [is] severe	البردُ قارسٌ
The cold was severe	كَانَ البردُ قارسًا
The cold will be severe	يَكُونُ البردُ قارسًا
The cold might be severe*	قَدْ يَكُونُ البردُ قارسًا*

* The use of قَدْ before the *present tense* expresses a probability or an element of doubt.

كَانَ may precede or follow the subject (المبتدأ) of a nominal sentence. In either case its **subject** is in the *nominative case* and the **predicate** is in the *accusative case* (see Unit 9).

يَكُون preceded by سَوْفَ or its abbreviation سَ, emphasizes the *future tense*:

We will be in Lebanon throughout the holiday

سَوْف نكون / سَنكون في لبنان طوال العطلة

The house will be ready next week

البيتُ سَيكون حاضرًا في الأسبوع القادم

2. كَانَ as an auxiliary verb

We have already seen in Units 12 and 13 that the *past tense* in Arabic expresses actions that are complete and it is translated into the *simple past tense* in English. The *present tense* in Arabic is equivalent to the *simple present tense* or the *present continuous tense*.

In order to express actions with more precision in relation to time, the verb

يَكُون / كَانَ is used in combination with the *present* or the *past te*ˌ
another verb.

(a) كَانَ with the *past tense* of a second verb is used to express the *past perfect tense:*

The secretary [m] had written the report

كَانَ السكرتيرُ قَدْ كَتَبَ التقريرَ

The particle قَدْ is usually added and is placed *directly before* the main verb with the subject placed *between* the two verbs.

The *past perfect* can also be expressed in Arabic by the use of بَعْدَ *after,* followed by a verb in the *past tense* preceded by the particle أَنْ:

I travelled after I had received a letter from the manager

سَافَرْتُ بَعْدَ أَنْ إِسْتَلَمْتُ رسالة من المدير

(b) كَانَ with the *present tense* of another verb is used to express a repeated act or a continuous action in the past, i.e. *past habitual* or *past continuous tense*:

Aziz used to go to the cafe everday day

كَانَ عزيز يَذْهَبُ إلى المقهى كلَّ يوم

Khadija was studying

كَانَتْ خديجة تَدْرُسُ

Using كَانَ with the *active participle* gives a similar meaning:

Aziz was sitting

كَانَ عزيز جَالِسًا

Aziz was sitting

كَانَ عزيز يَجْلِسُ

(c) The *present tense* of كَانَ (يَكُون) with the *past tense* of another verb is used to express the *future perfect*. Again it is usual to use the particle قَدْ:

After two days my brother will have arrived in Muscat

بعد يومين يَكُونُ أخي قَدْ وَصَلَ إلى مسقط

The conjugation of the verb يَكُونُ / كَانَ is shown in the table below:

	Past	Present			Imperative
		indicative	*subjunctive*	*jussive*	
I	كُنْتُ	أَكُونُ	أَكُونَ	أَكُنْ	
you [ms]	كُنْتَ	تَكُونُ	تَكُونَ	تَكُنْ	كُنْ
you [fs]	كُنْتِ	تَكُونِينَ	تَكُونِي	تَكُونِي	كُونِي
he	كَانَ	يَكُونُ	يَكُونَ	يَكُنْ	
she	كَانَتْ	تَكُونُ	تَكُونَ	تَكُنْ	
we	كُنَّا	نَكُونُ	نَكُونَ	نَكُنْ	
you [mp]	كُنْتُمْ	تَكُونُونَ	تَكُونُوا	تَكُونُوا	كُونُوا
they [mp]	كَانُوا	يَكُونُونَ	يَكُونُوا	يَكُونُوا	
you [fp]	كُنْتُنَّ	تَكُنَّ	تَكُنَّ	تَكُنَّ	كُنَّ
they [fp]	كُنَّ	يَكُنَّ	يَكُنَّ	يَكُنَّ	
you [md]	كُنْتُمَا	تَكُونَانِ	تَكُونَا	تَكُونَا	كُونَا
you [fd]	كُنْتُمَا	تَكُونَانِ	تَكُونَا	تَكُونَا	كُونَا
they [md]	كَانَا	يَكُونَانِ	يَكُونَا	يَكُونَا	
they [fd]	كَانَتَا	تَكُونَانِ	تَكُونَا	تَكُونَا	

Note that the third radical «ن» and that of the *past tense suffixes* for **we, they** *[fp]* and the *present tense suffixes* for **you** *[fp]* and **they** *[fp]* are written as a single «ن» with a *shadda*.

NON-SOUND VERBS فِعْلٌ غَيْرُ سَالِمٍ

The Doubled Verb الفِعْلُ المُضَعَّفُ

A doubled verb is one whose *second* and *third radicals* are *identical*. The conjugation is regular and is in accordance with the rules for sound verbs given in Units 12 and 13, except that the verb has two stems: a **contracted stem,** فِعّ, where the two radicals are written once with a *shadda,* and a **regular stem,** فعع, where the two radicals are written separately.

The **contracted stem** is used in both tenses and for those parts of the verb whenever:
(a) there is no verb suffix;
(b) the written verb suffix is preceded by a vowel.

In the *present tense* when the contracted stem is used, the vowel which would have been on the second radical is taken up by the first radical which was vowelless:

يَظُنُّ   for   يَظْنُنُ

he thinks

يَتِمُّ   for   يَتْمِمُ

he finishes

If the first radical is vowelled, as it is in the *past tense,* the vowel of the second radical is lost:

ظَنَّ   for   ظنَنَ

he doubted

The **regular stem** is used when the written verb suffix is preceded by a consonant.

The same rules for the formation of the *imperative* and the *passive,* which have already been given in Units 14 and 15, apply to doubled verbs.

Most doubled verbs take a فتحة for the second radical in the *past tense* and generally take a ضمّة as the vowel for the second radical in the *present tense*. However, a few verbs take a كسرة in the *present tense*:

يَشْكُكْنَ	شَكَكْتُ
they [fp] doubt	I doubted
يَشْدِدْنَ	شَدَدْتُ
they [fp] tie	I tied

A few doubled verbs take a كسرة as the second radical in the *past tense* and a فتحة in the *present tense*:

يَظْلَلْنَ	ظَلِلْتُ
they [fp] remain	I remained

In the *past tense* the contracted parts of all the different patterns are of the form... فَعَّ (apart from the 3rd person masculine plural where it is of the form فَعُّوا). Thus for the three verb patterns referred to above, we have:

Present Tense	Past Tense		
يَشُكُّ	شَكُّوا	شَكَّتْ	شَكَّ
he doubts	they [mp] doubted	she doubted	he doubted
يَشِدُّ	شَدُّوا	شَدَّتْ	شَدَّ
he ties	they [mp] tied	she tied	he tied
يَظَلُّ	ظَلُّوا	ظَلَّتْ	ظَلَّ
he remains	they [mp] remained	she remained	he remained

The conjugation of the verb ظَنَّ to *think* is shown in the following table:

	Past	Present			Imperative
		indicative	*subjunctive*	*jussive*	
I	ظَنَنْتُ	أَظُنُّ	أَظُنَّ	**أَظُنَّ** or أَظْنُنْ	
you [ms]	ظَنَنْتَ	تَظُنُّ	تَظُنَّ	**تَظُنَّ** or تَظْنُنْ	**ظُنَّ** or أُظْنُنْ
you [fs]	ظَنَنْتِ	تَظُنِّينَ	تَظُنِّي	تَظُنِّي	**ظُنِّي** or أُظْنُنِي
he	ظَنَّ	يَظُنُّ	يَظُنَّ	**يَظُنَّ** or يَظْنُنْ	
she	ظَنَّتْ	تَظُنُّ	تَظُنَّ	**تَظُنَّ** or تَظْنُنْ	
we	ظَنَنَّا	نَظُنُّ	نَظُنَّ	**نَظُنَّ** or نَظْنُنْ	
you [mp]	ظَنَنْتُم	تَظُنُّونَ	تَظُنُّوا	تَظُنُّوا	**ظُنُّوا** or أُظْنُنُوا
they [mp]	ظَنُّوا	يَظُنُّونَ	يَظُنُّوا	يَظُنُّوا	
you [fp]	ظَنَنْتُنَّ	تَظْنُنَّ	تَظْنُنَّ	تَظْنُنَّ	أُظْنُنَّ
they [fp]	ظَنَنَّ	يَظْنُنَّ	يَظْنُنَّ	يَظْنُنَّ	
you [md]	ظَنَنْتُمَا	تَظُنَّانِ	تَظُنَّا	تَظُنَّا	**ظُنَّا** or أُظْنُنَا
you [fd]	ظَنَنْتُمَا	تَظُنَّانِ	تَظُنَّا	تَظُنَّا	**ظُنَّا** or أُظْنُنَا
they [md]	ظَنَّا	يَظُنَّانِ	يَظُنَّا	يَظُنَّا	
they [fd]	ظَنَّتَا	تَظُنَّانِ	تَظُنَّا	تَظُنَّا	

The **regular stem** is used in the *past tense* for the 1st and 2nd persons, (**s, d and p**), and for the 3rd person feminine plural, and also in the *present tense* for the 2nd and 3rd persons feminine plural only.

Note that the *jussive mood* and the *imperative* have two forms for some persons. The most commonly used type, which is identical to the subjunctive mood, is shown in the table in **bold**.

The Hamzated Verbs الفِعْلُ المَهْمُوزُ

The hamzated verbs are of three groups according to whether the *hamza* is the *first radical* as in أَخَذَ *to take*, or the *second radical* as in رَأَسَ *to be in charge*, or the *third radical* as in بَدَأَ *to begin*.

Verbs with hamza as a first radical

These are conjugated as shown in the table below:

	Past	Present			Imperative
		indicative	*subjunctive*	*jussive*	
I	أَخَذْتُ	آخُذُ	آخُذَ	آخُذْ	
you [ms]	أَخَذْتَ	تَأْخُذُ	تَأْخُذَ	تَأْخُذْ	خُذْ
you [fs]	أَخَذْتِ	تَأْخُذِينَ	تَأْخُذِي	تَأْخُذِي	خُذِي
he	أَخَذَ	يَأْخُذُ	يَأْخُذَ	يَأْخُذْ	
she	أَخَذَتْ	تَأْخُذُ	تَأْخُذَ	تَأْخُذْ	
we	أَخَذْنَا	نَأْخُذُ	نَأْخُذَ	نَأْخُذْ	
you [mp]	أَخَذْتُمْ	تَأْخُذُونَ	تَأْخُذُوا	تَأْخُذُوا	خُذُوا
they [mp]	أَخَذُوا	يَأْخُذُونَ	يَأْخُذُوا	يَأْخُذُوا	
you [fp]	أَخَذْتُنَّ	تَأْخُذْنَ	تَأْخُذْنَ	تَأْخُذْنَ	خُذْنَ
they [fp]	أَخَذْنَ	يَأْخُذْنَ	يَأْخُذْنَ	يَأْخُذْنَ	
you [md]	أَخَذْتُمَا	تَأْخُذَانِ	تَأْخُذَا	تَأْخُذَا	خُذَا
you [fd]	أَخَذْتُمَا	تَأْخُذَانِ	تَأْخُذَا	تَأْخُذَا	خُذَا
they [md]	أَخَذَا	يَأْخُذَانِ	يَأْخُذَا	يَأْخُذَا	
they [fd]	أَخَذَتَا	تَأْخُذَانِ	تَأْخُذَا	تَأْخُذَا	

Notes

1. In the *present tense* 1st person singular, the initial *hamza* is prefixed by a *hamza*.

   The two are written together as an *alif* having a *madda*.

2. A peculiarity common to verbs أَكَلَ *to eat*, أَخَذَ *to take* and أَمَرَ *to command* is that the first radical *hamza* is dropped in the *imperative*:

كُلْ	خُذْ	مُرْ
eat!	*take!*	*command!*

In the *imperative* of other **Form I** verbs the *hamza* is dropped and is replaced by أُو for verbs with a characteristic **u-vowel** in the *present tense*, or إِي for verbs with a characteristic **i/a-vowel** in the *present tense*:

أَمَلَ / يَأْمُلُ	أُومُلْ	أُومُلِي	etc.
to hope for	hope! [ms]	hope! [fs]	
أَسَرَ / يَأْسِرُ	إِيسِرْ	إِيسِرِي	etc.
to capture	capture! [ms]	capture! [fs]	
أَلِفَ / يَأْلَفُ	إِيلَفْ	إِيلَفِي	etc.
to be acquainted	be acquainted! [ms]	be acquainted! [fs]	

Verbs with hamza as a second radical

These are conjugated regularly, as shown in the table below for the verb رَأَسَ to be in charge:

	Past	Present			Imperative
		indicative	*subjunctive*	*jussive*	
I	رَأَسْتُ	أَرْأَسُ	أَرْأَسَ	أَرْأَسْ	
you [ms]	رَأَسْتَ	تَرْأَسُ	تَرْأَسَ	تَرْأَسْ	إِرْأَسْ
you [fs]	رَأَسْتِ	تَرْأَسِينَ	تَرْأَسِي	تَرْأَسِي	إِرْأَسِي
he	رَأَسَ	يَرْأَسُ	يَرْأَسَ	يَرْأَسْ	
she	رَأَسَتْ	تَرْأَسُ	تَرْأَسَ	تَرْأَسْ	
we	رَأَسْنَا	نَرْأَسُ	نَرْأَسَ	نَرْأَسْ	
you [mp]	رَأَسْتُمْ	تَرْأَسُونَ	تَرْأَسُوا	تَرْأَسُوا	إِرْأَسُوا
they [mp]	رَأَسُوا	يَرْأَسُونَ	يَرْأَسُوا	يَرْأَسُوا	
you [fp]	رَأَسْتُنَّ	تَرْأَسْنَ	تَرْأَسْنَ	تَرْأَسْنَ	إِرْأَسْنَ
they [fp]	رَأَسْنَ	يَرْأَسْنَ	يَرْأَسْنَ	يَرْأَسْنَ	
you [md]	رَأَسْتُمَا	تَرْأَسَانِ	تَرْأَسَا	تَرْأَسَا	إِرْأَسَا
you [fd]	رَأَسْتُمَا	تَرْأَسَانِ	تَرْأَسَا	تَرْأَسَا	إِرْأَسَا
they [md]	رَأَسَا	يَرْأَسَانِ	يَرْأَسَا	يَرْأَسَا	
they [fd]	رَأَسَتَا	تَرْأَسَانِ	تَرْأَسَا	تَرْأَسَا	

The verb سَأَلَ *to ask* has **two forms** of the *jussive mood*; those shown in the table are regular. The alternative form has the *middle hamza* elided and its vowel taken up by the first radical, viz. أَسَلْ (1st person singular) تَسَلْ (2nd person *[ms]* and 3rd person *[fs]*), etc.

Thus we have an alternative form of the *imperative*, which is:

سَلْ، سَلِي، سَلَا، سَلُوا، سَلْنَ

	Past	Present			Imperative
		indicative	*subjunctive*	*jussive*	
I	سَأَلْتُ	أَسْأَلُ	أَسْأَلَ	أَسْأَلْ	
you [ms]	سَأَلْتَ	تَسْأَلُ	تَسْأَلَ	تَسْأَلْ	إِسْأَلْ
you [fs]	سَأَلْتِ	تَسْأَلِينَ	تَسْأَلِي	تَسْأَلِي	إِسْأَلِي
he	سَأَلَ	يَسْأَلُ	يَسْأَلَ	يَسْأَلْ	
she	سَأَلَتْ	تَسْأَلُ	تَسْأَلَ	تَسْأَلْ	
we	سَأَلْنَا	نَسْأَلُ	نَسْأَلَ	نَسْأَلْ	
you [mp]	سَأَلْتُمْ	تَسْأَلُونَ	تَسْأَلُوا	تَسْأَلُوا	إِسْأَلُوا
they [mp]	سَأَلُوا	يَسْأَلُونَ	يَسْأَلُوا	يَسْأَلُوا	
you [fp]	سَأَلْتُنَّ	تَسْأَلْنَ	تَسْأَلْنَ	تَسْأَلْنَ	إِسْأَلْنَ
they [fp]	سَأَلْنَ	يَسْأَلْنَ	يَسْأَلْنَ	يَسْأَلْنَ	
you [md]	سَأَلْتُمَا	تَسْأَلَانِ	تَسْأَلَا	تَسْأَلَا	إِسْأَلَا
you [fd]	سَأَلْتُمَا	تَسْأَلَانِ	تَسْأَلَا	تَسْأَلَا	إِسْأَلَا
they [md]	سَأَلَا	يَسْأَلَانِ	يَسْأَلَا	يَسْأَلَا	
they [fd]	سَأَلَتَا	تَسْأَلَانِ	تَسْأَلَا	تَسْأَلَا	

Verbs with hamza as a third radical

These are conjugated regularly, as shown in the table below for the verb بَدَأَ to begin:

	Past	Present			Imperative
		indicative	*subjunctive*	*jussive*	
I	بَدَأْتُ	أَبْدَأُ	أَبْدَأَ	أَبْدَأْ	
you [ms]	بَدَأْتَ	تَبْدَأُ	تَبْدَأَ	تَبْدَأْ	إِبْدَأْ
you [fs]	بَدَأْتِ	تَبْدَئِينَ	تَبْدَئِي	تَبْدَئِي	إِبْدَئِي
he	بَدَأَ	يَبْدَأُ	يَبْدَأَ	يَبْدَأْ	
she	بَدَأَتْ	تَبْدَأُ	تَبْدَأَ	تَبْدَأْ	
we	بَدَأْنَا	نَبْدَأُ	نَبْدَأَ	نَبْدَأْ	
you [mp]	بَدَأْتُمْ	تَبْدَؤُونَ	تَبْدَؤُوا	تَبْدَؤُوا	إِبْدَؤُوا
they [mp]	بَدَؤُوا	يَبْدَؤُونَ	يَبْدَؤُوا	يَبْدَؤُوا	
you [fp]	بَدَأْتُنَّ	تَبْدَأْنَ	تَبْدَأْنَ	تَبْدَأْنَ	إِبْدَأْنَ
they [fp]	بَدَأْنَ	يَبْدَأْنَ	يَبْدَأْنَ	يَبْدَأْنَ	
you [md]	بَدَأْتُمَا	تَبْدَآنِ	تَبْدَآ	تَبْدَآ	إِبْدَآ
you [fd]	بَدَأْتُمَا	تَبْدَآنِ	تَبْدَآ	تَبْدَآ	إِبْدَآ
they [md]	بَدَآ	يَبْدَآنِ	يَبْدَآ	يَبْدَآ	
they [fd]	بَدَأَتَا	تَبْدَآنِ	تَبْدَآ	تَبْدَآ	

Weak Verbs فِعْلٌ مُعْتَلٌّ

A weak verb is one which has as one of its radicals a واو or a ياء. Weak verbs are divided into three classes: (a) assimilated verbs; (b) hollow verbs; and (c) defective verbs.

Assimilated Verbs (فعل مثال)

These are verbs whose first radical is a واو or a ياء

A verb with واو as its **first radical,** as in وَصَلَ *to arrive,* is shown below:

	Past	Present			Imperative
		indicative	*subjunctive*	*jussive*	
I	وَصَلْتُ	أَصِلُ	أَصِلَ	أَصِلْ	
you [ms]	وَصَلْتَ	تَصِلُ	تَصِلَ	تَصِلْ	صِلْ
you [fs]	وَصَلْتِ	تَصِلِينَ	تَصِلِي	تَصِلِي	صِلِي
he	وَصَلَ	يَصِلُ	يَصِلَ	يَصِلْ	
she	وَصَلَتْ	تَصِلُ	تَصِلَ	تَصِلْ	
we	وَصَلْنَا	نَصِلُ	نَصِلَ	نَصِلْ	
you [mp]	وَصَلْتُمْ	تَصِلُونَ	تَصِلُوا	تَصِلُوا	صِلُوا
they [mp]	وَصَلُوا	يَصِلُونَ	يَصِلُوا	يَصِلُوا	
you [fp]	وَصَلْتُنَّ	تَصِلْنَ	تَصِلْنَ	تَصِلْنَ	صِلْنِ
they [fp]	وَصَلْنَ	يَصِلْنَ	يَصِلْنَ	يَصِلْنَ	
you [md]	وَصَلْتُمَا	تَصِلَانِ	تَصِلَا	تَصِلَا	صِلَا
you [fd]	وَصَلْتُمَا	تَصِلَانِ	تَصِلَا	تَصِلَا	صِلَا
they [md]	وَصَلَا	يَصِلَانِ	يَصِلَا	يَصِلَا	
they [fd]	وَصَلَتَا	تَصِلَانِ	تَصِلَا	تَصِلَا	

Notes for the verb وَصَلَ *to arrive*
1. Verbs with واو as their first radical are conjugated regularly in the *past tense.*
2. The *present active* and the *imperative* lose their واو. This irregularity is shown by verbs of this class whose *middle radical* in the *present* has كسرة, and also by many that take فتحة in the *present.* The واو is retained in the *present of the passive.*

A doubled verb with واو as its **first radical**, as in وَدَّ *to love*, is shown below:

	Past	Present			Imperative
		indicative	*subjunctive*	*jussive*	
I	وَدِدْتُ	أَوَدُّ	أَوَدَّ	أَوَدَّ or أَوْدَدْ	
you [ms]	وَدِدْتَ	تَوَدُّ	تَوَدَّ	تَوَدَّ or تَوْدَدْ	وَدَّ or إِيدَدْ
you [fs]	وَدِدْتِ	تَوَدِّينَ	تَوَدِّي	تَوَدِّي	وَدِّي
he	وَدَّ	يَوَدُّ	يَوَدَّ	يَوَدَّ or يَوْدَدْ	
she	وَدَّتْ	تَوَدُّ	تَوَدَّ	تَوَدَّ or تَوْدَدْ	
we	وَدِدْنَا	نَوَدُّ	نَوَدَّ	نَوَدَّ or نَوْدَدْ	
you [mp]	وَدِدْتُمْ	تَوَدُّونَ	تَوَدُّوا	تَوَدُّوا	وَدُّوا
they [mp]	وَدُّوا	يَوَدُّونَ	يَوَدُّوا	يَوَدُّوا	
you [fp]	وَدِدْتُنَّ	تَوْدَدْنَ	تَوْدَدْنَ	تَوْدَدْنَ	إِيدَدْنَ
they [fp]	وَدِدْنَ	يَوْدَدْنَ	يَوْدَدْنَ	يَوْدَدْنَ	
you [md]	وَدِدْتُمَا	تَوَدَّانِ	تَوَدَّا	تَوَدَّا	وَدَّا
you [fd]	وَدِدْتُمَا	تَوَدَّانِ	تَوَدَّا	تَوَدَّا	وَدَّا
they [md]	وَدَّا	يَوَدَّانِ	يَوَدَّا	يَوَدَّا	
they [fd]	وَدَّتَا	تَوَدَّانِ	تَوَدَّا	تَوَدَّا	

Notes for the verb وَدَّ *to love*

Verbs of this class are conjugated regularly and retain their واو in the *present tense*. The use of the contracted or regular stem is determined by the rules given for doubled verbs shown earlier in this unit. Verbs of this class are very rare.

A verb with ياء as its **first radical,** as in يَقِظَ *to be awake,* is shown below:

	Past	Present			Imperative
		indicative	*subjunctive*	*jussive*	
I	يَقِظْتُ	أَيْقَظُ	أَيْقَظَ	أَيْقَظْ	
you [ms]	يَقِظْتَ	تَيْقَظُ	تَيْقَظَ	تَيْقَظْ	إِيقَظْ
you [fs]	يَقِظْتِ	تَيْقَظِينَ	تَيْقَظِي	تَيْقَظِي	إِيقَظِي
he	يَقِظَ	يَيْقَظُ	يَيْقَظَ	يَيْقَظْ	
she	يَقِظَتْ	تَيْقَظُ	تَيْقَظَ	تَيْقَظْ	
we	يَقِظْنَا	نَيْقَظُ	نَيْقَظَ	نَيْقَظْ	
you [mp]	يَقِظْتُمْ	تَيْقَظُونَ	تَيْقَظُوا	تَيْقَظُوا	إِيقَظُوا
they [mp]	يَقِظُوا	يَيْقَظُونَ	يَيْقَظُوا	يَيْقَظُوا	
you [fp]	يَقِظْتُنَّ	تَيْقَظْنَ	تَيْقَظْنَ	تَيْقَظْنَ	إِيقَظْنِ
they [fp]	يَقِظْنَ	يَيْقَظْنَ	يَيْقَظْنَ	يَيْقَظْنَ	
you [md]	يَقِظْتُمَا	تَيْقَظَانِ	تَيْقَظَا	تَيْقَظَا	إِيقَظَا
you [fd]	يَقِظْتُمَا	تَيْقَظَانِ	تَيْقَظَا	تَيْقَظَا	إِيقَظَا
they [md]	يَقِظَا	يَيْقَظَانِ	يَيْقَظَا	يَيْقَظَا	
they [fd]	يَقِظَتَا	تَيْقَظَانِ	تَيْقَظَا	تَيْقَظَا	

Weak verbs of this type are conjugated regularly.

Hollow Verbs فِعْلٌ أَجْوَفٌ

A hollow verb is one having one of the weak letters واو or ياء as the **second radical.** The conjugation of hollow verbs falls into three groups.

Group 1: Verbs with medial واو, pattern **-a** in the *past tense* and **-u** in the *present*.

	Past	Present			Imperative
		indicative	*subjunctive*	*jussive*	
I	قُلْتُ	أَقُولُ	أَقُولَ	أَقُلْ	
you [ms]	قُلْتَ	تَقُولُ	تَقُولَ	تَقُلْ	قُلْ
you [fs]	قُلْتِ	تَقُولِينَ	تَقُولِي	تَقُولِي	قُولِي
he	قَالَ	يَقُولُ	يَقُولَ	يَقُلْ	
she	قَالَتْ	تَقُولُ	تَقُولَ	تَقُلْ	
we	قُلْنَا	نَقُولُ	نَقُولَ	نَقُلْ	
you [mp]	قُلْتُمْ	تَقُولُونَ	تَقُولُوا	تَقُولُوا	قُولُوا
they [mp]	قَالُوا	يَقُولُونَ	يَقُولُوا	يَقُولُوا	
you [fp]	قُلْتُنَّ	تَقُلْنَ	تَقُلْنَ	تَقُلْنَ	قُلْنَ
they [fp]	قُلْنَ	يَقُلْنَ	يَقُلْنَ	يَقُلْنَ	
you [md]	قُلْتُمَا	تَقُولاَنِ	تَقُولاَ	تَقُولاَ	قُولاَ
you [fd]	قُلْتُمَا	تَقُولاَنِ	تَقُولاَ	تَقُولاَ	قُولاَ
they [md]	قَالاَ	يَقُولاَنِ	يَقُولاَ	يَقُولاَ	
they [fd]	قَالَتَا	تَقُولاَنِ	تَقُولاَ	تَقُولاَ	

Notes for the verb قَالَ *to say*

1. *Present tense verbs* have واو between the first and final radicals with the exception of *you [fp]* and *they [fp]*.

2. In the *jussive*, the long vowel واو of the *indicative* changes to a short **u**-vowel when the verb has a vowelless final radical. Shortening of the long vowel does not occur if the verb has an attached suffix (see also Unit 13).

Group 2: Verbs with medial واو, **pattern -i** in the *past tense* and **-a** in the *present*.

	Past	Present			Imperative
		indicative	*subjunctive*	*jussive*	
I	خِفْتُ	أَخَافُ	أَخَافَ	أَخَفْ	
you [ms]	خِفْتَ	تَخَافُ	تَخَافَ	تَخَفْ	خَفْ
you [fs]	خِفْتِ	تَخَافِينَ	تَخَافِي	تَخَافِي	خَافِي
he	خَافَ	يَخَافُ	يَخَافَ	يَخَفْ	
she	خَافَتْ	تَخَافُ	تَخَافَ	تَخَفْ	
we	خِفْنَا	نَخَافُ	نَخَافَ	نَخَفْ	
you [mp]	خِفْتُمْ	تَخَافُونَ	تَخَافُوا	تَخَافُوا	خَافُوا
they [mp]	خَافُوا	يَخَافُونَ	يَخَافُوا	يَخَافُوا	
you [fp]	خِفْتُنَّ	تَخَفْنَ	تَخَفْنَ	تَخَفْنَ	خَفْنَ
they [fp]	خِفْنَ	يَخَفْنَ	يَخَفْنَ	يَخَفْنَ	
you [md]	خِفْتُمَا	تَخَافَانِ	تَخَافَا	تَخَافَا	خَافَا
you [fd]	خِفْتُمَا	تَخَافَانِ	تَخَافَا	تَخَافَا	خَافَا
they [md]	خَافَا	يَخَافَانِ	يَخَافَا	يَخَافَا	
they [fd]	خَافَتَا	تَخَافَانِ	تَخَافَا	تَخَافَا	

Notes for the verb خَافَ *to fear*
1. *Present tense verbs* have *alif* between the first and final radical, with the exception of *you [fp]* and *they [fp]*.
2. The *jussive* is formed by shortening the long vowel *alif* to فتحة when the verb has a vowelless final radical. Shortening of the long vowel does not occur if the verb has an attached suffix.

Verbs with medial واو not elided

A few verbs whose medial radical is واو of the form فَعِلَ, usually denoting physical defects, retain their واو and are conjugated regularly:

يَعْوَجَ عَوِجَ

was crooked

يَعْوَرُ عَوِرَ

was one-eyed

يَشْوَهُ شَوِهَ

was deformed

The واو is also retained in **Form IX** verbs, which denote colour or defect, and in some **Form VIII** and **X** verbs:

Form VIII	إِزْدَوَجَ	يَزْدَوِجُ
	paired	
Form IX	إِسْوَدَّ	يَسْوَدُّ
	was or became black	
Form IX	إِعْوَجَّ	يَعْوَجُّ
	was or became bent	
Form X	إِسْتَجْوَبَ	يَسْتَجْوِبُ
	he interrogated	

Group 3: Verbs with medial ياء, **pattern -a** in the *past tense* and **-i** in the *present*.

	Past	Present			Imperative
		indicative	*subjunctive*	*jussive*	
I	زِدْتُ	أَزِيدُ	أَزِيدَ	أَزِدْ	
you [ms]	زِدْتَ	تَزِيدُ	تَزِيدَ	تَزِدْ	زِدْ
you [fs]	زِدْتِ	تَزِيدِينَ	تَزِيدِي	تَزِيدِي	زِيدِي
he	زَادَ	يَزِيدُ	يَزِيدَ	يَزِدْ	
she	زَادَتْ	تَزِيدُ	تَزِيدَ	تَزِدْ	
we	زِدْنَا	نَزِيدُ	نَزِيدَ	نَزِدْ	
you [mp]	زِدْتُمْ	تَزِيدُونَ	تَزِيدُوا	تَزِيدُوا	زِيدُوا
they [mp]	زَادُوا	يَزِيدُونَ	يَزِيدُوا	يَزِيدُوا	
you [fp]	زِدْتُنَّ	تَزِدْنَ	تَزِدْنَ	تَزِدْنَ	زِدْنَ
they [fp]	زِدْنَ	يَزِدْنَ	يَزِدْنَ	يَزِدْنَ	
you [md]	زِدْتُمَا	تَزِيدَانِ	تَزِيدَا	تَزِيدَا	زِيدَا
you [fd]	زِدْتُمَا	تَزِيدَانِ	تَزِيدَا	تَزِيدَا	زِيدَا
they [md]	زَادَا	يَزِيدَانِ	يَزِيدَا	يَزِيدَا	
they [fd]	زَادَتَا	تَزِيدَانِ	تَزِيدَا	تَزِيدَا	

Notes for the verb زَادَ *to increase*
1. *Present tense verbs* have ياء between the first and final radical, with the exception of *you [fp]* and *they [fp]*.
2. The *jussive* is formed by shortening the long vowel ياء to كسرة when the verb has a vowelless final radical. Shortening of the long vowel does not occur if the verb has an attached suffix.

A fourth group of hollow verbs exists having a medial ياء, **pattern -i** in the *past* and **-a** in the *present*. Verbs belonging to this group, which are relatively uncommon, are conjugated in exactly the same manner as those of Group 2:

هَابَ   *he feared*   يَهَاب

Note that in the *past tense* of hollow verbs having a medial *alif*, the *alif* is dropped for those parts of the conjugation which have a verb suffix preceded by a consonant. The *alif* that is dropped is replaced by:

(i) A ضَمّة if the *present tense verb* has a واو:

قَالَ	يَقُولُ	قُلْتُ	قُلْنَا	قُلْتُمْ
he said	he says	I said	we said	you [mp] said

(ii) A كسرة if the *present tense verb* has an ألف or a ياء:

خَافَ	يَخَافُ	خِفْتُ	خِفْنَا	خِفْتُمْ
he feared	he fears	I feared	we feared	you [mp] feared

زَادَ	يَزِيدُ	زِدْتُ	زِدْنَا	زِدْتُمْ
he increased	he increases	I increased	we increased	you [mp] increased

(iii) A فتحة if the verb is a *derived* type:

Form IV	أَقَامَ	أَقَمْتُ	أَقَمْنَا	أَقَمْتُمْ
	he set up	I set up	we set up	you [mp] set up
Form VIII	إِعْتَادَ	إِعْتَدْتُ	إِعْتَدْنَا	إِعْتَدْتُمْ
	he was used to	I was used to	we were used to	you [mp] were used to
Form X	إِسْتَجَابَ	إِسْتَجَبْتُ	إِسْتَجَبْنَا	إِسْتَجَبْتُمْ
	he granted (a request)	I granted	we granted	you [mp] granted

The *imperative* of hollow verbs is formed according to the rules given in Unit 15.

The *passive* of all four groups of hollow verbs is identical for all parts:

Past passive

قِيلَ	خِيفَ	زِيدَ	هِيبَ
it was said	it was feared	it was increased	he was feared

Present passive

يُقَالُ	يُخَافُ	يُزَادُ	يُهَابُ
it is said	*it is feared*	*it is increased*	*he is feared*

Defective Verbs فِعْلٌ نَاقِصٌ

A defective verb is one whose third radical is واو or ياء.

Verbs with the Final Radical واو

Pattern -a in the *past tense* and **-u** in the *present* is shown below for the verb دَعَا *to call:*

	Past	Present			Imperative
		indicative	*subjunctive*	*jussive*	
I	دَعَوْتُ	أَدْعُو	أَدْعُوَ	أَدْعُ	
you [ms]	دَعَوْتَ	تَدْعُو	تَدْعُوَ	تَدْعُ	أُدْعُ
you [fs]	دَعَوْتِ	تَدْعِينَ	تَدْعِي	تَدْعِي	أُدْعِي
he	دَعَا	يَدْعُو	يَدْعُوَ	يَدْعُ	
she	دَعَتْ	تَدْعُو	تَدْعُوَ	تَدْعُ	
we	دَعَوْنَا	نَدْعُو	نَدْعُوَ	نَدْعُ	
you [mp]	دَعَوْتُمْ	تَدْعُونَ	تَدْعُوا	تَدْعُوا	أُدْعُوا
they [mp]	دَعَوْا	يَدْعُونَ	يَدْعُوا	يَدْعُوا	
you [fp]	دَعَوْتُنَّ	تَدْعُونَ	تَدْعُونَ	تَدْعُونَ	أُدْعُونَ
they [fp]	دَعَوْنَ	يَدْعُونَ	يَدْعُونَ	يَدْعُونَ	
you [md]	دَعَوْتُمَا	تَدْعُوَانِ	تَدْعُوَا	تَدْعُوَا	أُدْعُوَا
you [fd]	دَعَوْتُمَا	تَدْعُوَانِ	تَدْعُوَا	تَدْعُوَا	أُدْعُوَا
they [md]	دَعَوَا	يَدْعُوَانِ	يَدْعُوَا	يَدْعُوَا	
they [fd]	دَعَتَا	تَدْعُوَانِ	تَدْعُوَا	تَدْعُوَا	

Verbs with the final radical واو

Pattern -i in the **past tense** and **-a** in the **present** is shown below for the verb رَضِيَ *to approve:*

	Past	Present			Imperative
		indicative	*subjunctive*	*jussive*	
I	رَضِيْتُ	أَرْضَى	أَرْضَى	أَرْضَ	
you [ms]	رَضِيتَ	تَرْضَى	تَرْضَى	تَرْضَ	إِرْضَ
you [fs]	رَضِيتِ	تَرْضَيْنَ	تَرْضَيْ	تَرْضَيْ	إِرْضَيْ
he	رَضِيَ	يَرْضَى	يَرْضَى	يَرْضَ	
she	رَضِيَتْ	تَرْضَى	تَرْضَى	تَرْضَ	
we	رَضِينَا	نَرْضَى	نَرْضَى	نَرْضَ	
you [mp]	رَضِيتُمْ	تَرْضَوْنَ	تَرْضَوْا	تَرْضَوْا	إِرْضَوْا
they [mp]	رَضُوا	يَرْضَوْنَ	يَرْضَوْا	يَرْضَوْا	
you [fp]	رَضِيتُنَّ	تَرْضَيْنَ	تَرْضَيْنَ	تَرْضَيْنَ	إِرْضَيْنَ
they [fp]	رَضِينَ	يَرْضَيْنَ	يَرْضَيْنَ	يَرْضَيْنَ	
you [md]	رَضِيتُمَا	تَرْضَيَانِ	تَرْضَيَا	تَرْضَيَا	إِرْضَيَا
you [fd]	رَضِيتُمَا	تَرْضَيَانِ	تَرْضَيَا	تَرْضَيَا	إِرْضَيَا
they [md]	رَضِيَا	يَرْضَيَانِ	يَرْضَيَا	يَرْضَيَا	
they [fd]	رَضِيَتَا	تَرْضَيَانِ	تَرْضَيَا	تَرْضَيَا	

Verbs with the final radical ياء

Pattern -a in the *past tense* and -i in the *present* is shown below for the verb رَمَى *to throw:*

	Past	Present			Imperative
		indicative	*subjunctive*	*jussive*	
I	رَمَيْتُ	أَرْمِي	أَرْمِيَ	أَرْمِ	
you [ms]	رَمَيْتَ	تَرْمِي	تَرْمِيَ	تَرْمِ	إِرْمِ
you [fs]	رَمَيْتِ	تَرْمِينَ	تَرْمِي	تَرْمِي	إِرْمِي
he	رَمَى	يَرْمِي	يَرْمِيَ	يَرْمِ	
she	رَمَتْ	تَرْمِي	تَرْمِيَ	تَرْمِ	
we	رَمَيْنَا	نَرْمِي	نَرْمِيَ	نَرْمِ	
you [mp]	رَمَيْتُمْ	تَرْمُونَ	تَرْمُوا	تَرْمُوا	إِرْمُوا
they [mp]	رَمَوْا	يَرْمُونَ	يَرْمُوا	يَرْمُوا	
you [fp]	رَمَيْتُنَّ	تَرْمِينَ	تَرْمِينَ	تَرْمِينَ	إِرْمِينَ
they [fp]	رَمَيْنَ	يَرْمِينَ	يَرْمِينَ	يَرْمِينَ	
you [md]	رَمَيْتُمَا	تَرْمِيَانِ	تَرْمِيَا	تَرْمِيَا	إِرْمِيَا
you [fd]	رَمَيْتُمَا	تَرْمِيَانِ	تَرْمِيَا	تَرْمِيَا	إِرْمِيَا
they [md]	رَمَيَا	يَرْمِيَانِ	يَرْمِيَا	يَرْمِيَا	
they [fd]	رَمَتَا	تَرْمِيَانِ	تَرْمِيَا	تَرْمِيَا	

Verbs with the final radical ياء

Pattern -i in the *past tense* and *-a* in the *present* is shown below for the verb لَقِيَ *to meet:*

	Past	Present			Imperative
		indicative	*subjunctive*	*jussive*	
I	لَقِيتُ	أَلْقَى	أَلْقَى	أَلْقَ	
you [ms]	لَقِيتَ	تَلْقَى	تَلْقَى	تَلْقَ	إِلْقَ
you [fs]	لَقِيتِ	تَلْقَيْنَ	تَلْقَيْ	تَلْقَيْ	إِلْقَيْ
he	لَقِيَ	يَلْقَى	يَلْقَى	يَلْقَ	
she	لَقِيَتْ	تَلْقَى	تَلْقَى	تَلْقَ	
we	لَقِينَا	نَلْقَى	نَلْقَى	نَلْقَ	
you [mp]	لَقِيتُمْ	تَلْقَوْنَ	تَلْقَوْا	تَلْقَوْا	إِلْقَوْا
they [mp]	لَقُوا	يَلْقَوْنَ	يَلْقَوْا	يَلْقَوْا	
you [fp]	لَقِيتُنَّ	تَلْقَيْنَ	تَلْقَيْنَ	تَلْقَيْنَ	إِلْقَيْنَ
they [fp]	لَقِينَ	يَلْقَيْنَ	يَلْقَيْنَ	يَلْقَيْنَ	
you [md]	لَقِيتُمَا	تَلْقَيَانِ	تَلْقَيَا	تَلْقَيَا	إِلْقَيَا
you [fd]	لَقِيتُمَا	تَلْقَيَانِ	تَلْقَيَا	تَلْقَيَا	إِلْقَيَا
they [md]	لَقِيَا	يَلْقَيَانِ	يَلْقَيَا	يَلْقَيَا	
they [fd]	لَقِيَتَا	تَلْقَيَانِ	تَلْقَيَا	تَلْقَيَا	

Notes about defective verbs

1. The verbs رَضِيَ and لَقِيَ are conjugated regularly in the past tense except for the 3rd person masculine plural where the ي is omitted.

   This part of the *past tense* of all defective verbs loses its final weak radical.

   The *present tense* for *you [mp]* and *they [mp]* drops the final weak radical before the suffix is added. This feature is shared by all defective verbs.

2. The ى at the end of a *past tense* verb changes to ـيْ (-ay) when a **verb suffix** preceded by a consonant or the «ا» of *they [md]* is added:

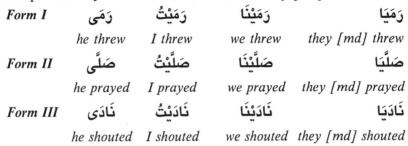

Form I	رَمَى	رَمَيْتُ	رَمَيْنَا	رَمَيَا
	he threw	I threw	we threw	they [md] threw
Form II	صَلَّى	صَلَّيْتُ	صَلَّيْنَا	صَلَّيَا
	he prayed	I prayed	we prayed	they [md] prayed
Form III	نَادَى	نَادَيْتُ	نَادَيْنَا	نَادَيَا
	he shouted	I shouted	we shouted	they [md] shouted

The «ا» at the end of verbs changes to a وْ (-aw) under the same suffixation:

دَعَا	دَعَوْتُ	دَعَوْنَا	دَعَوْتُمْ
he invited	I invited	we invited	you [mp] invited

3. The *jussive* for those persons which take no suffix, *you [mp]* and *they [mp]*, lose the final weak radical (و for the verb دَعَا and ى for the verbs لَقِيَ and رَضِيَ) and is replaced by the corresponding short vowel.

4. Defective verbs ending in *alif* (ا or ى) lose their final weak radical in the *past tense* for the 3rd person feminine singular, 3rd person feminine dual, and as stated in note 1 above, the 3rd person masculine plural:

دَعَا	دَعَتْ*	دَعَتَا	دَعَوْا
he invited	she invited	they [fd] invited	they [mp] invited
رَمَى	رَمَتْ*	رَمَتَا	رَمَوْا
he threw	she threw	they [fd] threw	they [mp] threw

* The weak letter ى reappears in the *passive tense*:

دُعِيَتْ	دُعِيَتَا	رُمِيَتْ	رُمِيَتَا

Derived verbs ending in ى lose their ى for the same part of the conjugation:

سَمَّى	سَمَّتْ	سَمَّتَا	سَمُّوا
he named	she named	they [fd] named	they [mp] named

5. In the *past tense* all derived forms of defective verbs change their final radical into ى for the 3rd person masculine singular:

Form I	Form VIII	Form X
دَعَا	إِدَّعَى	إِسْتَدْعَى
he called	he maintained	he summoned
Form I	Form III	Form IV
لَقِيَ	لاقَى	أَلْقَى
he met	he came across	he threw off

The *present indicative* of the derived forms of defective verbs ends in ـِي except for **Forms V** and **VI** where the ending is ـَى:

Form II	Form III	Form IV	Form V
يُسَمِّي	يُنَادِي	يُلْقِي	يَتَلَقَّى
he names	he shouts	he throws off	he receives
Form VI	Form VII	Form VIII	Form X
يَتَبَارَى	يَنْقَضِي	يَشْتَرِي	يَسْتَثْنِي
he vies	it passes [time]	he buys	he excepts

The *passive* of all four groups of defective verbs is identical for all parts.

Past passive

دُعِيَ	رُضِيَ	رُمِيَ	لُقِيَ
he was invited	it was approved	it was thrown	he was met

Present passive

يُدْعَى	يُرْضَى	يُرْمَى	يُلْقَى
he is called	it is approved	it is thrown	he is met

Doubly Weak Verbs

The verb رَأَى *he saw* has a medial *hamza* and a final يَاء:

	Past	Present			Imperative
		indicative	*subjunctive*	*jussive*	
I	رَأَيْتُ	أَرَى	أَرَى	أَرَ	
you [ms]	رَأَيْتَ	تَرَى	تَرَى	تَرَ	رَ
you [fs]	رَأَيْتِ	تَرَيْنَ	تَرَيْ	تَرَيْ	رَيْ
he	رَأَى	يَرَى	يَرَى	يَرَ	
she	رَأَتْ	تَرَى	تَرَى	تَرَ	
we	رَأَيْنَا	نَرَى	نَرَى	نَرَ	
you [mp]	رَأَيْتُمْ	تَرَوْنَ	تَرَوْا	تَرَوْا	رَوْا
they [mp]	رَأَوْا	يَرَوْنَ	يَرَوْا	يَرَوْا	
you [fp]	رَأَيْتُنَّ	تَرَيْنَ	تَرَيْنَ	تَرَيْنَ	رَيْنَ
they [fp]	رَأَيْنَ	يَرَيْنَ	يَرَيْنَ	يَرَيْنَ	
you [md]	رَأَيْتُمَا	تَرَيَانِ	تَرَيَا	تَرَيَا	رَيَا
you [fd]	رَأَيْتُمَا	تَرَيَانِ	تَرَيَا	تَرَيَا	رَيَا
they [md]	رَأَيَا	يَرَيَانِ	يَرَيَا	يَرَيَا	
they [fd]	رَأَتَا	تَرَيَانِ	تَرَيَا	تَرَيَا	

Verbs, as in the verb وَقَى *he guarded,* have their first and third radicals as weak letters:

	Past	Present			Imperative
		indicative	*subjunctive*	*jussive*	
I	وَقَيْتُ	أَقِي	أَقِيَ	أَقِ	
you [ms]	وَقَيْتَ	تَقِي	تَقِيَ	تَقِ	قِ
you [fs]	وَقَيْتِ	تَقِينَ	تَقِي	تَقِي	قِي
he	وَقَى	يَقِي	يَقِيَ	يَقِ	
she	وَقَتْ	تَقِي	تَقِيَ	تَقِ	
we	وَقَيْنَا	نَقِي	نَقِيَ	نَقِ	
you [mp]	وَقَيْتُمْ	تَقُونَ	تَقُوا	تَقُوا	قُوا
they [mp]	وَقَوْا	يَقُونَ	يَقُوا	يَقُوا	
you [fp]	وَقَيْتُنَّ	تَقِينَ	تَقِينَ	تَقِينَ	قِينَ
they [fp]	وَقَيْنَ	يَقِينَ	يَقِينَ	يَقِينَ	
you [md]	وَقَيْتُمَا	تَقِيَانِ	تَقِيَا	تَقِيَا	قِيَا
you [fd]	وَقَيْتُمَا	تَقِيَانِ	تَقِيَا	تَقِيَا	قِيَا
they [md]	وَقَيَا	يَقِيَانِ	يَقِيَا	يَقِيَا	
they [fd]	وَقَتَا	تَقِيَانِ	تَقِيَا	تَقِيَا	

112

Verbs, as in the verb رَوَى *he related,* have their second and third radicals as weak letters:

	Past	Present			Imperative
		indicative	*subjunctive*	*jussive*	
I	رَوَيْتُ	أَرْوِي	أَرْوِيَ	أَرْوِ	
you [ms]	رَوَيْتَ	تَرْوِي	تَرْوِيَ	تَرْوِ	إِرْوِ
you [fs]	رَوَيْتِ	تَرْوِينَ	تَرْوِي	تَرْوِي	إِرْوِي
he	رَوَى	يَرْوِي	يَرْوِيَ	يَرْوِ	
she	رَوَتْ	تَرْوِي	تَرْوِيَ	تَرْوِ	
we	رَوَيْنَا	نَرْوِي	نَرْوِيَ	نَرْوِ	
you [mp]	رَوَيْتُمْ	تَرْوُونَ	تَرْوُوا	تَرْوُوا	إِرْوُوا
they [mp]	رَوَوْا	يَرْوُونَ	يَرْوُوا	يَرْوُوا	
you [fp]	رَوَيْتُنَّ	تَرْوِينَ	تَرْوِينَ	تَرْوِينَ	إِرْوِينَ
they [fp]	رَوَيْنَ	يَرْوِينَ	يَرْوِينَ	يَرْوِينَ	
you [md]	رَوَيْتُمَا	تَرْوِيَانِ	تَرْوِيَا	تَرْوِيَا	إِرْوِيَا
you [fd]	رَوَيْتُمَا	تَرْوِيَانِ	تَرْوِيَا	تَرْوِيَا	إِرْوِيَا
they [md]	رَوَيَا	يَرْوِيَانِ	يَرْوِيَا	يَرْوِيَا	
they [fd]	رَوَتَا	تَرْوِيَانِ	تَرْوِيَا	تَرْوِيَا	

Notes

1. The verb رَأَى is conjugated in the *past tense* like the verb رَمَى, but in the *present tense* the medial *hamza* and its carrier are lost and its vowel is taken up by the first radical.

2. The *hamza* of رَأَى becomes a *madda* when a pronoun suffix is attached to the verb:

رَآهُ	رَآهَا	رَآهُمْ
he saw him	*he saw her*	*he saw them [m]*

3. The *imperative* is not used.

4. The verb وَقَـــــى *he guarded* combines the features of assimilated and defective verbs. In the *past tense* it is conjugated like the verb رَمَى. In the *present tense* it follows the patterns for the conjugation of the assimilated (e.g. وَصَلَ) and the defective (e.g. رَمَى) verbs.

5. In verbs like رَوَى, in which the second and third radicals are weak letters, the second radical is treated as a consonant and is retained throughout the conjugated parts.

DERIVED FORMS OF THE VERB الفِعْلُ المَزِيدُ

The vast majority of verbs, in their simplest forms, are built up from roots each of which consists of *three radicals*. From this basic form of the verb, المجرَّد, *nine forms*, in theory, can be derived, المزيد, by modifying the stem by the addition of one, two or three letters, accompanied in some cases by a change in the internal vowelling, in a specific manner. Accompanied with this modification of the verb there is a variation in meaning. Traditionally the *basic form* is assigned the Roman numeral **I** and the *derived forms* the numerals **II-X**.

Arab grammarians use the letters ل، ع، ف for discussing word patterns. The ف stands for the *first radical* of the root, the ع stands for the *second radical* and the ل stands for the *third*.

This method of indicating patterns is known in Arabic as: الميزان الصّرفيّ

Form I This is the basic form consisting of the three root consonants. This form has three sub-varieties:

فَعَلَ	فَعِلَ	فَعُلَ
كَسَرَ	عَلِمَ	حَسُنَ
he broke	*he learned*	*he became fine*

Form II فَعَّلَ

This form denotes the intensity of the action or a causative action and is made by doubling the second radical of the base root with a *shadda:*

	I	II	
he broke	كَسَرَ	كَسَّرَ	*he smashed*
he cut	قَطَعَ	قَطَّعَ	*he cut to pieces*
he studied	دَرَسَ	دَرَّسَ	*he taught*
he learned	عَلِمَ	عَلَّمَ	*he taught*

115

Notes

1. The middle radical of the *past tense* always takes an -**a** vowel, while that of the *present tense* takes an -**i** vowel:

   يدرِّس *he teaches*   تدرِّس *she teaches*

2. The prefixes of the *present tense* of this form take a -**u** vowel instead of an -**a** vowel.

3. Verbs in this group are identical in conjugation with sound quadriliteral verbs.

Form III   فَاعَلَ

This form usually expresses the action of a verb to another person.

	I		III	
he wrote	كَتَبَ		كَاتَبَ	*corresponded*

This pattern is formd by adding an *alif* after the first root consonant:

he struggled	كَافَحَ	*he met*	قَابَلَ

Note that the prefixes of the *present tense* of Form III verbs take a -**u** vowel instead of an -**a** vowel.

Verbs of this form, like those of Form II, are conjugated in the same manner as those of sound quadriliteral verbs.

Note that the *past passive* of these verbs is formed by changing the long vowel ألِف into واو:

صَاحَبَ *he kept company*   صُوحِبَ *he was accompanied*

Form IV   أَفْعَلَ

	I		IV	
he knew	عَلِمَ		أَعْلَمَ	*he informed*
he got up	نَهَضَ		أَنْهَضَ	*he awakened someone*
he sat	جَلَسَ		أَجْلَسَ	*he seated someone*

This form is made by prefixing the base root by a *hamza* carried on an *alif* (أ) and omitting the *fatha* on the first consonant.

This form is quite common and is generally causative.

The prefixes of the *present tense* of this form, like those of Forms II and III, take a **-u** vowel instead of an **-a** vowel. This feature, which characterizes Forms II, III and IV, occurs in verbs in which there is **one** additional letter to those in the base root.

Verbs of this form are conjugated regularly in the *past tense*, but in the *present* the initial «أ» is dropped:

يُعْلِم	*he informs*	تُعْلِم	*she informs*

Form V   تَفَعَّلَ

This form in general has the meaning of the action indicated by Form II being done in the interests of the subject (reflexive of Form II):

	II	**V**	
he taught	عَلَّمَ	تَعَلَّمَ	*he learned, studied*

Form V is made by prefixing تَ to Form II.

Form V verbs are conjugated regularly, but note that the *present stem* is vowelled فتحة all through:

يَتَعَلَّم	*he learns*	تَتَعَلَّم	*she learns*

The *past passive* is formed by changing the vowel of both the first and second consonants to ضمّة and that of the penultimate consonant to كسرة:

تَسَلَّمَ	*he received*	تُسُلِّمَ	*it was received*

Form VI   تَفَاعَلَ

This form has the meaning of the action indicated by Form III in association with others (reflexive of Form III):

	III	**VI**	
offered	نَاوَلَ	تَنَاوَلَ	*received*
wrote to	كَاتَبَ	تَكَاتَبَ	*corresponded*
assisted	عَاوَنَ	تَعَاوَنَ	*co-operated*

Form VI is made by prefixing تَ to Form III.

Verbs of this form are conjugated regularly, but **note** that the *present stem*, like that of Form V, is vowelled فتحة all through:

يَتَعَاوَن *he co-operates*   تَتَعَاوَن *she co-operates*

The *past passive* is formed by changing the vowel of both the first and second consonants to ضمّة, that of the penultimate consonant to كسرة, and the medial ألف into واو:

تَبَادَلَ   *he exchanged*   تُبُودِلَ   *it was exchanged*

Form VII إنْفَعَلَ

This form usually has a passive or reflexive meaning of Form I and is *intransitive*:

	I		VII	
he broke	كَسَرَ		إنْكَسَرَ	*it was broken*
he turned over	قَلَبَ		إنْقَلَبَ	*it was turned over*

Form VII is made by prefixing إنْ to Form I.

Verbs of **Forms VII - X** all have initial «إ» in their *past stem* as no word in Arabic can begin with a vowelless consonant. This «إ» is dropped in the present stem of all four forms.

Verbs of this form are conjugated regularly in the *past tense*.

Present tense

أنْبَسِط *I become happy*   يَنْبَسِط *he becomes happy*

The *past passive* is formed by making the vowel of the initial «إ» and the first consonant of the root ضمّة and that of the penultimate consonant كسرة:

Past Active   **Past Passive**

إنْقَلَبَ   *it was turned over*   أُنْقُلِبَ

118

The *passive* is not often used because verbs of this form generally have a passive sense.

Form VIII إِفْتَعَلَ

This form is similar to Form VII in that it also has a reflexive meaning of Form I.

	I	**VIII**	
he came near	قَرَبَ	إِقْتَرَبَ	he approached
he collected	جَمَعَ	إِجْتَمَعَ	he assembled
he looked	نَظَرَ	إِنْتَظَرَ	he waited

This form is made by the addition of تَ after the first consonant of the base form, dropping the -a vowel of the first consonant and adding «إ» as a prefix.

This form is conjugated regularly, but the «إ» is elided in the *present tense*:

أَنْتَظِر   I wait   يَنْتَظِر   he waits

The *past passive* is formed by changing the vowel of both the prefixed «إ» and the infixed «ت» to ضمّة and that of the penultimate consonant to كسرة:

إِنْتَخَبَ   he elected   أُنْتُخِبَ   he was elected

Note the following phonetic changes of the *infixed* «ت»:
(a) The infixed «ت» changes to «د» if the root verb begins with د، ذ or ز:

دَعَمَ	he supported	إِدَّعَمَ	was supported
دَعَا	he called	إِدَّعَى *	he maintained
ذَخَرَ	he preserved	إِدَّخَرَ / إِذَّخَرَ	he preserved
زَجَرَ	he rebuked	إِزْدَجَرَ	was restrained

* Note the change of the final *alif* in the Form I verb to «ى» in the Form VIII verb. All derived forms of defective verbs end in «ى» for the 3rd person singular past tense.

(b) The infixed «تَ» becomes «طَ» if the root verb begins with one of the emphatic letters ض، ص or ط:

صَحَبَ	he was a friend	إِصْطَحَبَ	he accompanied
ضَرَّ	he harmed	إِضْطَرَّ	he compelled
طَرَدَ	he drove away	إِطَّرَدَ	flowed uninterruptedly

(c) The infixed «تَ» becomes «ظَ» if the root verb begins with the emphatic letter ظ:

ظَلَمَ	he oppressed	إِظَّلَمَ	he suffered oppression

(d) If the root verb begins with واو this is assimilated with the infixed «تَ»:

وَجَهَ	he belonged to the notables	إِتَّجَهَ	he tended
وَحَدَ	he was alone	إِتَّحَدَ	united with

(e) Some verbs which have an initial همزة assimilate this with the infixed «تَ»:

أَخَذَ	he took	إِتَّخَذَ	he took up [for himself]
أَزَرَ	he surrounded	إِتَّزَرَ	he wrapped himself

Form IX   إِفْعَلَّ

This form is rare and is used only with verbs denoting colours and physical defects:

became red	إِحْمَرَّ	became crooked / bent	إِعْوَجَّ

Form IX is formed by prefixing «اِ» to the Form I stem, doubling the final radical with a *shadda*, and dropping the vowel of the first radical.

This form is conjugated in the same manner as a doubled verb.

Form X   إِسْتَفْعَلَ

The meaning of this form can sometimes be interpreted as the causative or reflexive of Form IV.

	IV		X	
he informed	أَعْلَمَ		إِسْتَعْلَمَ	he enquired

أَعْمَلَ *he put to work*   إِسْتَعْمَلَ *he used*

أَخْبَرَ *he informed*   إِسْتَخْبَرَ *he asked about*

Form X is formed by prefixing إِسْتَ to the base root and dropping the vowel of the first radical.

Verbs of this form are conjugated regularly, but the «إ» is dropped in the *present*:

Past	**Present**
إِسْتَعْمَلْتُ	يَسْتَعْمِل
I used	*he uses*
إِسْتَعْمَلْتَ	تَسْتَعْمِل
you (ms) used	*she uses*

The *past passive* is formed in a similar manner to that of Form VIII:

إِسْتَعْمَلَ *he used*   أُسْتُعْمِلَ *it was used*

Notes

1. Not all the theoretically possible derived forms of a given root actually exist. A decision as to which form is real or imagined can be reached by reference to a dictionary.
2. There are a number of derived forms in use where the root form does not exist.
3. The comments made regarding the effect of the various forms on meaning are shown only to give some useful suggestions and are not intended to be absolute.

THE VERBAL NOUN المَصْدَرُ

The verbal noun, also referred to as *gerund* or *noun of action,* expresses the idea or action of the corresponding verb. The meaning of the verbal noun has no bearing on when the action took place and it therefore may express the past, the present or the future. A simple verb may have one or more of some forty verbal noun patterns. The better dictionaries give the verbal noun for each verb. Sometimes more than one verbal noun is given for the same verb and these may have the same or different meanings. It is best for students to learn these patterns as they come across them.

A few of the most common patterns for the verbal noun of the *simple verb* are shown in the table below:

[Note: the use of ف، ع، ل to depict patterns is outlined in Unit 18: Derived Verbs.]

Pattern		Example		
Verb	**Verbal Noun**	**Verb**	**Verbal Noun**	**Notes**
فَعَلَ	فَعْل	ضَرَبَ *he beat, struck* حَمِدَ *he praised*	ضَرْب *beating* حَمْد *praise*	This pattern relates especially to *transitive* verbs of the form shown.
فَعِلَ	فَعْل			
فَعِلَ	فَعَل	عَجِبَ *he was astonished*	عَجَب *astonishment*	This pattern occurs in verbs denoting a **temporary state.**
فَعَلَ	فُعُول	نَهَضَ *he got up* زَهَرَ *he shined, shone*	نُهُوض *getting up* زُهُور *flowers*	This pattern occurs in *intransitive* verbs of the form shown.

Pattern		Example		
Verb	Verbal Noun	Verb	Verbal Noun	Notes
	فِعَالة	نَابَ *he represented* صَنَعَ *he made*	نِيَابة *representation* صِنَاعة *industry*	This pattern occurs especially in verbs denoting **an office** or **trade**.
فَعَلَ	فُعَال	سَعَلَ *he coughed* زَكَمَ *he caught cold*	سُعَال *coughing* زُكَام *bad cold*	This pattern occurs especially to *intransitive verbs* of the form shown denoting **illness**.
فَعَلَ	فَعِيل	هَدَرَ *it rolled* [thunder] *it surged* [sea]	هَدِير *roar* *surge*	This pattern occurs especially with *intransitive* verbs denoting **sound**.
فَعَلَ	فَعَلاَن	خَفَقَ *it throbbed*	خَفَقَان *throbbing*	This pattern occurs in *intransitive* verbs denoting a **disturbance**.

A number of the verbs listed above have more than one verbal noun.

Some verbs form their verbal noun with a prefix «م». A verbal noun of this type is called مصدر ميمي. The verbs listed below have more than one verbal noun:

غَفَرَ	*he forgave*	مَغْفِرَة	*forgiveness*
ذَمَّ	*he blamed*	مَذَمَّة	*blame*
وَعَدَ	*he promised*	مَوْعِد	*appointment*
ذَهَبَ	*he went*	مَذْهَب*	*belief/ideology*

* ذَهَاب is a 2nd verbal noun with the meaning *"going"*.

123

The verbal noun of a *simple doubled verb* uses the contracted form and is of the pattern فَعّ:

ظَنَّ	*he thought*	ظَنّ	*opinion/idea*
شَكَّ	*he doubted*	شَكّ	*a doubt*
وَدَّ	*he loved*	وَدّ	*loving*

The verbal noun of *sound quadriliteral verbs* is of the pattern فَعْلَلَة:

تَرْجَمَ	*he translated*	تَرْجَمَة	*translation*
طَنْطَنَ	*he rang, hummed*	طَنْطَنَة	*humming, jingle*

Verbal Nouns of Derived Verbs

The verbal nouns of derived verbs fall into fewer patterns than those of the simple verb.

Form II verbal nouns are mostly of the pattern تَفْعِيل or تَفْعِلَة or both:

دَبَّرَ	تَدْبِير
he made plans	*planning*

The pattern تَفْعِلَة is used if the *last radical* of the verb is a هَمزة، واو or ياء:

هَنَّأَ	تَهْنِئَة
he congratulated	*congratulation*
نَمَّى	تَنْمِيَة
he made grow	*expansion*
سَمَّى	تَسْمِيَة
he named	*designation*

Form III verbal nouns may be either of the pattern مُفَاعَلَة or of the pattern فِعَال:

حَاجَجَ	جِجَاج	شَارَكَ	مُشَارَكَة
he disputed	*dispute*	*he shared*	*partnership*

A few verbs take both forms:

كَافَحَ	كِفَاح	مُكَافَحَة
he struggled	*struggle*	*struggle*

Form IV verbal nouns are of the pattern إِفْعَال:

أَحْسَنَ	إِحْسَان
he did well	*charity*

Form V verbal nouns are of the pattern تَفَعُّل:

تَعَلَّمَ	تَعَلُّم
he learned	*learning*

Form VI verbal nouns are of the pattern تَفَاعُل:

تَبَادَلَ	تَبَادُل
he exchanged [views]	exchange [of views]

Note that in unvowelled text the verbal noun of this form derived from a sound verb does not differ from the 3rd person singular masculine **past tense**. The student should be able to differentiate between the verb and the verbal noun from the context.

If the third radical of the base verb is واو or يَاء, Form VI verbs have a verbal noun of the pattern تَفَاعٍ (التَّفَاعِي)

تَرَاضَى	(التَّرَاضِي) تَرَاضٍ
came to terms	*mutual consent*

Form VII verbal nouns are of the pattern إِنْفِعَال:

إِنْقَلَبَ	إِنْقِلَاب
it became overturned	*overthrow*

Form VIII verbal nouns are of the pattern إِفْتِعَال:

إِنْتَظَرَ	إِنْتِظَار
he waited	*waiting*

Form IX verbal nouns are of the pattern إِفْعِلَال:

إِحْمَرَّ   إِحْمِرَار

became red   *reddening*

Form X verbal nouns are of the pattern إِسْتِفْعَال:

إِسْتَعْمَلَ   إِسْتِعْمَال

he used   *use, application*

The verbal noun may act as a noun or as a verb. The most common use of the verbal noun is when it is used *without the definite article in a construct phrase* (إضافة) as in **ex. 1, 2, 4** and **5** below:

1. the rejoicing of the successful	فَرَحُ الناجِحِ
2. spreading knowledge	نَشْرُ العِلْمِ
3. his spreading knowledge	نَشْرُه العِلْمَ
4. Protection of the homeland is a duty	حِمايَةُ الوطنِ واجبٌ
5. He came to visit the institute of arts	جاءَ لِزِيَارةِ معهدِ الفنونِ
6. The search for oil is still going on	ما زال البَحْثُ عن البترول مستمرًّا
7. noted progress [or advance]	تَقَدُّمٌ ملحوظٌ
8. love of the pious of [the] *virtue and* [the] *uprightness*	حُبُّ التَّقي الفضيلةَ والإستقامةَ

Notes

In **ex. 1** the verbal noun (فَرَح) is in a construct state with its subject.

In **ex. 2** the verbal noun (نَشْر) is in a construct state with its object (العِلْم) and the latter is in the *genitive case*. However:

In **ex. 3** when the verbal noun has taken a pronoun suffix, the object (العِلْم) is in the *accusative case* (compare with **ex. 8** below).

In **ex. 8** the verbal noun has an object (فضيلة), thus showing a verbal element. The subject (التَّقي) is in a construct phrase.

Ex. 8 may also be constructed using the preposition لِ:

حُبُّ التَّقي لِلفضيلةِ والإستقامةِ

The *present tense verb* when it is *preceded* by the particle أَنْ can be replaced by the verbal noun, as shown below:

She wanted to cooperate with the charitable organizations

كانت تريد أَنْ تَتَعاوَنَ مع الجمعيات الخيرية

كانت تريد التَّعاوُنَ مع الجمعيات الخيرية

Verbal nouns, like nouns in general, take pronoun suffixes:

What happened after their [going out]?   ماذا حدث بعد خُرُوجِهِمْ؟

The Absolute Object (Absolute Accusative) المَفْعُولُ المُطْلَقُ

A feature of the Arabic language is the habit of using verbs with their own
verbal noun in the same sentence. The verb may be in the *past* or the *present*
tense.

1. The sea became rough [a rough]	هاجَ البحرُ هِياجًا
2. He triumphed [a triumph]	إنْتَصَرَ إنْتِصارًا
3. I visited the sick twice [two visits]	زُرْتُ المريضَ زِيارَتَيْنِ
4. He triumphed greatly	إنْتَصَرَ إنْتِصارًا عظيمًا
5. The price of property [real estate] *rose greatly*	
إرْتَفَعَ ثمنُ العقارِ إرْتِفاعًا كبيرًا	
6. He smiled the smile of the winner	إبْتَسَمَ إبْتِسامَ الفائزِ
7. He was treated well	عُومِلَ مُعامَلَةً طيّبةً
8. Splendid performance!	فَوْزًا باهِرًا!

In each of these sentences the *object* of the verb is a verbal noun
corresponding to the verb in the sentence. In such a construction the object
is called the **absolute object**.

Notes

In **ex. 1 and 2** the absolute object is used *without* an adjective and its purpose
 is for *emphasis*.

In **ex. 3** the absolute object shows the *number* of times the verb performed
 the action.

In **ex. 4** the verb, directly followed by its verbal noun and *qualified by* an
 adjective, gives an *adverbial* meaning.

In **ex. 4, 5, 6, 7** and **8** the absolute object is used for *specification*. This comes about either by the use of adjectives as in **ex. 4, 5, 7** and **8** or by إضافة, as in **ex. 6**. In this example the alternative verbal noun إِبْتِسَامَة may be used.

In **ex. 7** the absolute object is used with the *passive verb*.

In **ex. 8** the verb is *omitted* as it is perceived.

THE ACTIVE AND PASSIVE PARTICIPLES

إِسْمُ الفَاعِلِ وإِسْمُ المَفْعُولِ

The Active Participle إِسْمُ الفَاعِلِ

The active participle is a noun denoting the **"doer"** of the action. It is the equivalent in English of **-or** or **-er** at the end of the noun, as in *vendor* or *seller*.

The active participle can also be used to describe someone in the process of **"doing"** the verb (i.e. an action which is, **or** was, incomplete at the time):

she was living كانت سَاكِنَة

Form I *sound verbs* are of the pattern فَاعِل:

حَارِس *guard* from the verb حَرَسَ *he guarded*

Verbs whose first radical is واو also form their active participle after this pattern:

he stood	وَقَفَ	*standing*	وَاقِف
he trusted	وَثِقَ	*trusting/confident*	وَاثِق

The active participle of the derived forms is formed from its corresponding *present active* by replacing its prefix by (مُ) and placing a كسرة on the penultimate consonant. The exception to the above is **Form IX**, which takes a فتحة

Form II	يُدَرِّس	*he teaches*	مُدَرِّس	*teacher*
Form III	يُسَافِر	*he travels*	مُسَافِر	*traveller*
Form IV	يُسْلِم	*become a Muslim*	مُسْلِم	*Muslim*
Form V	يَتَحَمَّس	*to be overzealous*	مُتَحَمِّس	*enthusiast*
Form VI	يَتَنَاصَح	*to be loyal*	مُتَنَاصِح	*loyal, sincere*
Form VII	يَنْقَلِب	*to turn into*	مُنْقَلِب	*turned over*
Form VIII	يَجْتَهِد	*he works hard*	مُجْتَهِد	*diligent*

Form IX	يَحْمَرّ	to blush		مُحَمَرّ	blushing
Form X	يَسْتَقْبِل	to meet		مُسْتَقْبِل	receiver
Quadriliteral	يُتَرْجِم	he translates		مُتَرْجِم	translator

The Active Participle of Hollow Verbs

The active participle of a hollow verb is of the pattern فَائِل. This differs from the pattern فَاعِل for Form I sound verbs only in the *middle radical*. It is formed by changing the *middle radical* ألف of the *perfect verb* into a همزة:

Second radical واو:

		Root		
قَامَ	he got up	قوم	standing	قَائِم
قَادَ	he led	قود	leader	قَائِد

Second radical ياء:

		Root		
سَارَ	he walked	سير	walker	سَائِر
فَاضَ	it overflowed	فيض	abundant	فَائِض

The Active Participle of Defective Verbs

A defective verb is a verb having one of the weak letters واو or ياء as its *third radical*. The active participle is of the pattern فَاعٍ:

Third radical واو:

		Root		
دَعَا	he invited	دعو	inviter	دَاعٍ
رَجَا	he hoped	رجو	hoping	رَاجٍ

Third radical ياء:

		Root		
جَرَى	it flowed	جري	flowing	جَارٍ
رَمَى	he threw	رمي	thrower	رَامٍ

[see Unit 1]

The Active Participle of Doubled Verbs

The active participle of a doubled verb is of the pattern فَاعّ where the *second* and *third radicals* are assimilated:

شَكَّ   *he doubted*   شَاكّ   *sceptical*

دَلَّ   *he indicated*   دالّ   *showing*

The active participle, like other nouns, may be used with or without the definite article, has both genders and is declined. It generally takes the *sound plural* (see Unit 4).

The active participle is used a great deal as an **adverb of manner** (see Unit 21).

The active participle may be used as a noun, but it also retains some of the characteristics of a verb:

The ruler is honest   الحاكِمُ عادلٌ

the science teacher   مُدَرِّسُ العلومِ

Worry is a harmful disturbance [to its owner]

القلقُ إضطرابٌ ضَارٌّ صاحِبَهُ

Notes

In **ex. 2** the active participle مُدَرِّسُ is used as a noun and is followed by a genitive.

In **ex. 3** ضَارٌّ is the active participle of the doubled verb ضَرَّ and is used as an adjective to the noun preceding it. The active participle is doing the action of the verb and taking the object صَاحِبَهُ.

For other uses of the active participle, see Unit 16 and Unit 21.

The Passive Participle إِسْمُ المَفْعُولِ

The passive participle is a noun and is the recipient of the action of a verb. It is the equivalent in English of **-ed** or **-en** at the end of a noun, as in *repaired* or *fallen*.

In *sound three-radical verbs* it is formed on the pattern of مَفْعُول:

مَكْتُوب *written, letter* is the passive participle of the verb كَتَبَ *he wrote.*

Verbs with an initial radical واو also form their passive participle after this pattern:

وَصَلَ   *he connected*   مَوْصُول   *tied*

These are a few other patterns for the passive participle of *sound three-radical verbs:*

فَعِيل :   قَتِيل   *killed* [m and f]   ذَبِيح   *slaughtered* [m and f]

The passive participle of the derived verbs are formed from the **passive present tense** by replacing its prefix by (مُ):

Form II	يُكَسَّر	مُكَسَّر
	to be smashed	*smashed*
Form X	يُسْتَعْمَر	مُسْتَعْمَر
	to be colonized	*colonized*

The patterns for the active and passive participles for the derived verbs are shown below for comparison:

Forms	Active Participle	Passive participle
II	مُفَعِّل	مُفَعَّل
III	مُفَاعِل	مُفَاعَل
IV	مُفْعِل	مُفْعَل
V	مُتَفَعِّل	مُتَفَعَّل
VI	مُتَفَاعِل	مُتَفَاعَل
VII	مُنْفَعِل	مُنْفَعَل
VIII	مُفْتَعِل	مُفْتَعَل
IX	مُفْعَلّ	[does not exist]
X	مُسْتَفْعِل	مُسْتَفْعَل
Quadriliteral	مُتَرْجِم	مُتَرْجَم

Thus the only difference between the active and the passive participles of a *strong derived verb* is the vowel on the penultimate consonant. It is كسرة in the active participle and a فتحة in the passive participle.

Form IX is an exception as it has a فتحة in the active participle.

Passive Participle of Hollow Verbs

For verbs whose second radical is واو, the واو of the pattern مَفْعُول is dropped:

قَالَ	becomes	مَقُول
he said		*speech*
صَانَ	becomes	مَصُون
he preserved		*well-kept*

For verbs whose second radical is ياء, the واو of the pattern مَفْعُول is dropped:

بَاعَ	becomes	مَبِيع
he sold		*what is sold*
هَابَ	becomes	مَهِيب
he feared		*dreadful*

Passive Participle of Defective Verbs

Verbs whose third radical is واو follow the pattern مَفْعُول. The two واو are written as one with a *shadda:*

دَعَا	becomes	مَدْعُوّ
he invited		*guest*

For verbs whose third radical is ياء, the واو of the pattern مَفْعُول is changed into ياء. The two ياء are written as one with a *shadda:*

رَضِيَ	becomes	مَرْضِيّ
he approved		*afforded satisfaction*

The passive participle of a *doubled verb* is of the pattern مَفْعُول:

| شَكَّ | he doubted | becomes | مَشْكُوك | dubious |
| حَبَّ | he loved | becomes | مَحْبُوب | beloved |

Note how the second and third consonants are now no longer assimilated but expanded and the verb is treated as the pattern فَعَعَ

The passive participle may be used with or without the definite article, has both genders and is declined. It generally takes the *sound plural*. In syntax the passive participle takes the place of the passive verb in the manner that the active participle takes the place of the active verb.

Examples:

1. The honest man is respected   الرجلُ الصادقُ مُحْتَرَمٌ

2. The palace is fortified with a high fence

القصرُ مُحَصَّنٌ بسورٍ عالٍ

3. After his graduation the student was appointed an employee in the Ministry of Justice

بعد تخرُّج الطالب من الجامعة عُيِّن مُوَظَّفًا في وزارةِ العدلِ

Notes

In ex. 1 مُحْتَرَم is a passive participle of the **Form VIII** verb إِحْتَرَمَ he honoured.

In ex. 2 مُحَصَّن is a passive participle of the **Form II** verb حَصَّنَ he fortified.

In ex. 3 مُوَظَّف is a passive participle of the **Form II** verb وَظَّفَ he employed.

The Noun of Place and Time إِسْمُ المَكَانِ والزَّمَانِ

The noun of place and time denotes the place or time of an action. It is formed from the verb according to the following patterns.

مَفْعِل: This pattern is formed from:

(a) *sound verbs* which have كسرة in the *present tense*:

| يَرْجِع | to return | مَرْجِع | source |

يَجْلِس	to sit down	مَجْلِس	council
يَنْزِل	to take lodgings	مَنْزِل	house

(b) verbs having واو as their *first radical* and which take كسرة in the *present tense* usually take this form:

وَقَفَ	يَقِف	he stands still	مَوْقِف	stopping place
وَسَمَ	يَسِم	he brands	مَوْسِم	season, time of year
وَعَدَ	يَعِد	he promises	مَوْعِد	appointment

Some verbs which take فتحة in the *present tense* also take this form:

وَضَعَ	يَضَع	he places	مَوْضِع	place

مَفْعَل: This pattern is formed from:

(a) *sound verbs* which have فتحة in the *present tense*:

يَصْنَع	he manufactures	مَصْنَع	factory
يَلْعَب	he plays	مَلْعَب	playground
يَسْبَح	he swims	مَسْبَح	swimming pool

(b) *hamzated verbs* which have فتحة in the *present tense* usually have their noun of place/time on this pattern:

يَبْدَأ	to begin	مَبْدَأ	starting point
يَأْمَن	to be safe	مَأْمَن	place of safety
يَلْجَأ	to take refuge	مَلْجَأ	sanctuary

Verbs which have ضمّة in the *present tense* (with certain exceptions) also form their noun of place/time on the pattern of مَفْعَل:

يَنْظُر	he views	مَنْظَر	a view
يَقْعُد	he sits	مَقْعَد	a seat
يَخْرُج	he goes out	مَخْرَج	an exit

Exceptions

تَشْرُق	it rises [sun]	مَشْرِق	place of sunrise
تَغْرُب	it sets [sun]	مَغْرِب	place, time of sunset
يَسْجُد	he prostrates himself	مَسْجِد	mosque

مَفْعَلَة: No generalization can be made as to which verb forms this pattern:

زَرَعَ	he planted	مَزْرَعَة	farm
قَبَر	he buried	مَقْبَرَة	cemetery
دَرَسَ	he studied	مَدْرَسَة	school

Hollow verbs form their noun of place as follows:

Medial واو

		Root		
نَامَ	he slept	نوم	place to sleep	مَنَام
زَارَ	he visited	زور	place to visit	مَزَار

Medial ياء

		Root		
ضَاقَ	it was narrow	ضيق	strait	مَضِيق
طَارَ	it flew	طير	airport	مَطِير or مَطَار

Verbs which have واو or ياء as their *third radical* form their noun of place on the pattern shown:

جَرَى	it flowed	مَجْرى	water course
رَمَى	he threw	مَرْمَى	goal
رَعَى	grazed	مَرْعَى	grazing land

In **doubled verbs** the contracted stem is used for these nouns:

حَطَّ	مَحَطّ	مَحَطّة
set down, put	a stopping place	a station

136

حَلَّة	مَحَلّ	مَحَلّ
a city district	a place	stayed [at a place]

مَحَجّة	مَحَجّ	حَجّ
destination of pilgrimage	destination of journey	made a pilgrimage

Note that a verb may have two nouns of place/time. These may have the same or different meanings:

مِيعَاد	مَوْعِد	وَعَدَ
a promise	appointment	he promised

مَكْتَبَة	مَكْتَب	كَتَبَ
bookshop, library	office	he wrote

مِيلاد	مَوْلِد	وَلَدَ
birthday	birth place, anniversary	gave birth

The nouns of place and time of **Forms II - X** have the same patterns as the corresponding passive participles of these forms:

Form II	خَيَّمَ	مُخَيَّم
	he camped	camping ground

Form VIII	إِعْتَقَلَ	مُعْتَقَل
	was put under arrest	detention centre

Form X	إِسْتَشْفَى	مُسْتَشْفَى
	he was cured	hospital

The context will make it clear which one of the three nouns (passive participle, noun of place or time) is referred to.

The Noun of Instrument إِسْمُ الآلَةِ

This noun denotes the instrument used in an action and is formed according to the following patterns:

مِفْعَال

| نَظَرَ | he viewed | مِنْظَار | binoculars |
| حَرَثَ | he ploughed | مِحْرَاث | plough |

مِفْعَلَة

| طَرَقَ | he banged | مِطْرَقَة or مِطْرَق | hammer |
| مَسَحَ | he wiped off | مِمْسَحَة or مِمْسَح | dust cloth |

مِفْعَل

| بَرَدَ | he filed | مِبْرَد | file |
| سَحَجَ | he scraped off | مِسْحَج | plane |

There are a number of tools or instruments whose names do not conform to the above patterns:

| سِكِّينة | شَوْكة | مُنْخَل | فَأْس |
| knife | fork | sieve | hatchet |

THE ACCUSATIVE النَّصْبُ

Throughout the previous units, and particularly in Unit 3, the use of the accusative is discussed whenever appropriate. In this unit the following topics which take the accusative are explained:

1. Adverbs ظَرْف
2. Circumstantial Clauses حال
3. The Accusative of Specification التَّمْييز

Adverbs

These are of two types:

(a) Adverbs of Place ظرف مكان   (b) Adverbs of Time ظرف زمان

Adverbs of Place

يمينًا	*on the right*	يسارًا	*on the left*
داخلاً	*inside*	خارجًا	*outside*

See also Adverbs of Place in Units 7 and 10.

Adverbs of Time

اليومَ	*today* [**not** "the day"]	أمسَا	*yesterday*
مساءَ أمسٍ	*yesterday evening*	مساءً	*in the evening*
صباحًا	*in the morning*	غَدًا	*tomorrow*
الليلةَ	*tonight* [**not** "the night"]	ليلةَ أمسٍ	*last night*
وقتًا طويلاً	*long time*	أيّامًا	*days*
أخيرًا	*recently, finally*	سنويًّا	*annually*

The **ordinal numbers** when used adverbially are *indefinite* and in the *accusative case*:

firstly أوّلاً   *secondly* ثانيًا   *thirdly* ثالثًا

Circumstantial Clauses (Determination of Condition)

الحَال والجُمْلَة الحَالِيَّة

In such clauses the *indefinite active participle*, *passive participle* or the *verbal noun* is used to determine the condition of the noun to which it relates صاحب الحال:

He travelled equipped	سافر مُجَهَّزًا
They arrived one by one	وصلوا فردًا فردًا
He arrived riding his bicycle	وصل راكبًا دراجتَه

Another way of expressing حَال is by the use of a preposition:

Zaid came on his horse	جاء زيد على فرسِهِ

A circumstantial clause is sometimes referred to as an **Adverb of Manner**:

He looked at him amazed	نظر إليه متعجِّبًا
He continued saying	إستمرَّ قائلاً
The debate continued for long last night	

إستمرّت المناقشة طويلاً ليلةَ أمسِ

Adverb of Purpose

I rose in honour of the teacher	قمتُ إكرامًا للمعلّم

Discussion took place between the responsible [officials] *to maintain the peace in the area*

جرى تباحث بين المسؤولين إحتفاظًا للسلامِ في المنطقة

The verbal noun in these two examples shows the purpose or aim for which the action was performed.

The Accusative of Specification التَّمْيِيز

Consider the sentence below:

Zaid bought a kilogram [of] *sugar*	اشترى زيد كيلوغرامًا سكّرًا

The meaning of this sentence would be incomplete if the word سكّرًا, *sugar,* was omitted, even though the sentence is gramatically complete as it contains its essential elements: the verb, the subject and the object. The word سكّرًا in this sentence is called تمييز as it **specifies** that a kilogram of sugar was bought and **not** some other item, e.g. meat or vegetables. **It is always indefinite.**

Here, the word "kilogram" is referred to as مُمَيِّز *mumayyiz* (distinguishing). The *mumayyiz* can be of several types:

(a)   Units of Weights: *gramme* جرام or غرام *kilogram* كيلوجرام *ton* طَنّ رَطْل varies in weight **dependent** on the region from c. 449g to c. 2.56 kg.

(b)   Units of Length: *metre* مِتْر *yard* يارْدَة *foot* قَدَم *kilometre* كِيلُومِتْر *mile* مِيل
ذِراع varies in length **dependent** on the region from c. 0.58 m to c. 0.8 m.

(c)   Units of Area: *square metre* مِتْر مُرَبَّع *hectare* هِكْتَار *acre* فَدّان

(d)   Units of Volume: *litre* لِتْر *barrel* بَرْمِيل

(e)   Numbers.

Examples:

1. Zaid bought رطل of sugar	اشترى زيد رطلاً سكّرًا
2. She bought ذراع of woolly material	اشتَرت ذراعًا صوفًا
3. The farmer sowed an acre of wheat	زرع الفلاّح فدّانًا قمحًا
4. The family consumed a litre of milk	استهلكت الأسرة لتْرًا حليبًا
5. In the school there are twenty teachers	في المدرسة عشرون مدرّسًا

The case governing the numbers and counted nouns is discussed fully in Unit 29.
In the above examples the تمييز is in the *accusative case*.

Ex. 1–4 can be reconstructed as shown below:

اشترى زيد رطلاً من سكّرٍ   or   اشترى زيد رطلَ سكّرٍ

The تمييز is now in the *genitive case*.

Now consider these sentences (literal translation in English):

The summer resort was good [**in regard** to the air] طاب المصيفُ هواءً

Iron is more than copper in hardness [**in regard** to hardness]
الحديد أكثر من النحاس صلابةً

The Empty Quarter is the most intense of areas in heat
[**in regard** to heat] الربع الخالي من أشدّ المناطق حرارةً

In these examples the *mumayyiz* is absent.

This type of تمييز is also indefinite and is **always** in the *accusative case*.

THE RELATIVE ADJECTIVE اِسْمُ النِّسْبَةِ

(The Formation of Adjectives from Nouns)

Consider these words:

	adjective		noun	
international	عالَمِيّ		عالَم	world
Arabic	عربيّ		عرب	Arab
Egyptian	مصريّ		مصر	Egypt
scientific	عِلمِيّ		عِلم	science
golden	ذهبِيّ		ذهب	gold

The change of each of these nouns into its relative adjective involves the addition of يّ, preceded by كسرة, at the end of the noun. This method of changing a noun into its adjective is referred to as النسب, the noun is called المنسوب or إسم النسبة, the derived adjective is known as المنسوب إلَيْه, and the ي as ياء النسب. The شدّة over the ي makes *no difference* to its pronunciation.

Not all nouns can be changed in this way to form relative adjectives. Those nouns referring to countries, cities, businesses and some nouns used to form colours (both expanded upon later in this unit) are likely to be treated in this way. The following are some of the more common rules governing the change of a noun to its relative adjective:

1. If a noun does *not end in* ة, ا or ى, the adjective is formed by adding ي as shown above.

2. If a noun ends in ة or ألف, these letters and the فتحة preceding them are dropped before the ي is added:

	adjective		noun	
commercial	تجاريّ		تجارَة	commerce
ministerial	وزاريّ		وزارَة	ministry
American	أميركيّ		أميرَكا	America
Canadian	كنديّ		كندَا	Canada

143

3. If a **proper noun** is prefixed with the definite article «ال» it *loses* this in the formation of the *indefinite adjective:*

	adjective	noun	
Kuwaiti	كويتِيّ	الكويت	Kuwait
Bahraini	بحرينِيّ	البحرين	Bahrain
Sudanese	سودانِيّ	السودان	Sudan
Jordanian	أردنِيّ	الأردن	Jordan
Yemeni	يمنِيّ	اليمن	Yemen
Moroccan	مغربِيّ	المغرب	Morocco
Pakistani	باكستانِيّ	الباكستان	Pakistan

4. If a noun ends with ألف and is preceded by a ي, then both these letters are dropped before the ي is added:

	adjective	noun	
African	أفريقِيّ	أفريقيَا	Africa
Russian	روسِيّ	روسيَا	Russia
Turkish	تركِيّ	تركيَا	Turkey
British	بريطانِيّ	بريطانيَا	Britain
Syrian	سورِيّ	سوريَا	Syria

5. If a noun ends in ى this is changed into و before the ي is added, and the و becomes a **dipthong**:

spiritual, abstract	مَعْنَوِيّ	مَعْنَى	meaning

6. If a noun ends in «اء», the ء is dropped and a و is added before the ي (the ألف may or may not be dropped):

	adjective	noun	
wintry	شتوِيّ	شتاء	winter
heavenly	سماوِيّ	سماء	heaven, sky
desert-like	صحراوِيّ	صحراء	desert

Note that there are a number of words that *do not* conform to **rule 6** and where the همزة at the end of the noun is retained. This is particularly the case when the همزة is present in the root:

	adjective		noun
building	بِنائِيّ	بِناء	*building*
nourishing	غِذائِيّ	غِذاء	*nourishment*
sky blue	سَمائِيّ	سماء	*sky*

There are a large number of adjectives of this type ending in (ياء النسب) «ي» which are derived from their nouns in an irregular manner:

	adjective		noun
rustic, rural	قَرَوِيّ	قَرْيَة	*village*
bedouin, nomadic	بدوِيّ	بادية	*semi-desert, steppe*
spiritual	روحانِيّ	روح	*spirit*

Colours أَلْوَان

Colours in Arabic are either **basic** or **secondary**.

Basic Colours

Both the *dual forms* tabled here are used in speech and are the written form of the **accusative and genitive cases** (for the formation of the **nominative case**, see Unit 3: Case Endings).

Note: the (feminine dual and plural) have «و» instead of a final «ء».

f. plural	f. dual	feminine	m. plural	m. dual	masculine	colour
سَوْداوات	سَوْداوَيْن	سَوْداء	سُود	أَسْوَدَيْن	أَسْوَد	*black*
بَيْضاوات	بَيْضاوَيْن	بَيْضاء	بِيض	أَبْيَضَيْن	أَبْيَض	*white*
حَمْراوات	حَمْراوَيْن	حَمْراء	حُمْر	أَحْمَرَيْن	أَحْمَر	*red*
خَضْراوات	خَضْراوَيْن	خَضْراء	خُضْر	أَخْضَرَيْن	أَخْضَر	*green*
زَرْقاوات	زَرْقاوَيْن	زَرْقاء	زُرْق	أَزْرَقَيْن	أَزْرَق	*blue*

f. plural	f. dual	feminine	m. plural	m. dual	masculine	colour
صَفْراوات	صَفْراوَيْن	صَفْراء	صُفْر	أَصْفَرَيْن	أَصْفَر	yellow
سَمْراوات	سَمْراوَيْن	سَمْراء	سُمْر	أَسْمَرَيْن	أَسْمَر *	brown, tawny

*أَسْمَر is not regarded as a basic colour but is treated as such.

Secondary Colours

These colours are formed by adding the *adjective ending* ي (ياء النسب) to the name of the *natural object* to form the **masculine**, e.g. rose-coloured (rosy) وردِيّ = ي ِ + ورد

The *feminine* is formed by changing the final ي into يَّة, e.g. وردِيّ becomes وردِيَّة

masculine	colour	masculine	colour
برتقالِيّ	orange	زمرّدِيّ	emerald
قرنفلِيّ	pink/carnation	بنِّيّ	brown/coffee
أرجوانِيّ	purple	قرمزِيّ	crimson/scarlet
بنفسجِيّ	violet	رمادِيّ	grey/ash
برونزِيّ	bronze	ذهبِيّ	gold
نحاسِيّ	copper	فضِّيّ	silver

N.B. *light* فاتِح   *dark* غامِق or قاتِم

Countries and Peoples نِسْبة
(Singular, Dual and Plural)

Both the duals and the sound masculine plural endings tabled here are used in speech and are the written form of the accusative and genitive cases. (For the nominative case see Unit 3: Case Endings).

FP = (ـِيّات)	F DUAL = (ـِيّتَيْن)	FS = (ـِيّة)	MP = (ـِيّين)	M DUAL = (ـِيّيْن)	MS = (ـِيّ)
ending = iyaat	ending = iyatayn	ending = iya	ending = iyiin	ending = iyayn	ending = ii

N.B. Austria النِّمْسا   China الصِّين   Ethiopia الحَبَشة   Greece اليُونان   Hungary المَجَر   Mexico المَكْسيك

INTERROGATIVE PRONOUNS أَدَوَاتُ الإِسْتِفْهَام

أَ، هَلْ، مَنْ، مَا، مَاذَا، أَيّ، أَيَّة، مَتَى، أَيْنَ، كَيْفَ، كَمْ

Particles of Affirmation and Negation

أَحْرُفُ الجَوَابِ: نَعَمْ، أَجَلْ، بَلَى، لاَ، كَلَّا

There are very many colloquial variations to these words used throughout the Arabic-speaking world, but these are the correct words used in *writing* and in *formal discourse*.

All interrogative pronouns, with the exception of أَيّ and أَيَّة, and **particles of affirmation and negation** are *invariable*.

أَ : This particle is prefixed to the first word of the interrogative sentence. It is used before *verbs, indefinite nouns, pronouns* and *proper names*:

Did Umar travel?	أَسَافَر عمر؟
Yes, Umar travelled.	نَعَمْ سَافر عمر

نَعَمْ (or the less frequently used alternative for *yes* أَجَلْ) by itself would also suffice as an answer, meaning, e.g. *Yes, he travelled.*

بَلَى *yes* is used as an answer to **negative** questions.

كَلَّا /لاَ   *No*

When the answer is a negative, لاَ or its equivalent كَلَّا, is a sufficient answer in Arabic, meaning, e.g: *No, he did not travel.*

A combination of «أ» and أَمْ *or* is used to ask questions about **alternatives** the answer to which must be one of the two names:

Did Hamid win or did Majid? أَحميدٌ فاز أَمْ مجيدٌ؟

Negative Questions

A combination of the particle «أَ» and the negative particle لَمْ، لاَ or مَا, or the negating verb لَيْسَ, introduce a negative question:

Haven't I told you [ms]?	أَلَمْ أَقلْ لَكَ؟
Isn't that so?	أَلَيْسَ كذلك؟
Isn't this your [ms] house?	أَلَيْسَ هذا بيتكَ؟
Did you [ms] not send it [ms]?	أَمَا أرسلتَهُ؟
Should we not have ascertained the correctness of this news?	أَلاَ يجب علينا أنْ نتحقق من صحّة هذا الخبر؟

هَلْ This is a particle used to introduce interrogative sentences of the type:

Are you a student?	هَلْ أَنت طالب؟
Yes, I am a student.	نَعَمْ، أَنا طالب.
Is he a teacher?	هَلْ هو مدرِّس؟
No, he is an engineer.	لاَ، هو مهندس.
Did Aziz succeed?	هَلْ نجح عزيز؟
Yes, Aziz succeeded.	نَعَمْ، نجح عزيز.

مَنْ (*WHO?*) refers to **people only**:

Who is this?	مَنْ هذا؟
Who is she?	مَنْ هي؟
Who ate with you [fs]?	مَنْ أَكلَ معكِ؟

Note that مَنْ is pronounced as مَنِ when it is followed by a word beginning with «ال»:

which one?	مَنِ الَّذي؟

مَا and مَاذا (*WHAT?*) refers to **things**.

مَا as an interrogative is used before *nouns, personal pronouns, demonstratives* and *verbs*.

مَاذَا is used before *verbs.*

What is your name? [f]	مَا إِسمكِ؟
What is this? [m]	مَا هذا؟
What did you drink? [ms]	مَا شربتَ؟
What is your [fs] opinion on this subject?	مَا رأيكِ في هذا الموضوع؟
What did you buy? [ms]	مَاذَا إِشتريتَ؟

مَاذَا may be preceded by بِ, becoming بِمَاذَا (**in what?** or **about what?**):

About what does the teacher advise his pupils?

بِمَاذَا ينصح المعلّم تلاميذه؟

مَا has other uses which include:

(a) as a negating particle (see Unit 24);
(b) as a relative pronoun (see Unit 11);
(c) in exclamatory expressions (أسلوب التعجّب):

How delicious the taste of this date is!	مَا أحلى طعم هذا التمر!
What God wills!	مَا شاء اللَّه!

[an expression used to express astonishment]

أَيّ *(WHICH?)* *[m]* and أَيَّة *(WHICH?)* *[f]:* are used for both **people and things.**

(a) These are treated as nouns and *must agree* with the noun following them in gender.

(b) أَيّ and أَيَّة are *declinable.*

(c) The following noun is **singular**, **indefinite** and in the **genitive case**:

Which book did you [ms] read?	أَيّ كتاب قرأتَ؟
Which girl did you [ms] see?	أَيَّةَ بنتٍ رأيتَ؟

أَيّ / أَيَّة may be preceded by a preposition, as in:

About what did the pupil [m] ask his teacher?

عَنْ أَيِّ شيءٍ سأل التلميذ معلّمه؟

مَتَى *(WHEN?)* is used with **verbs** both in the past and in the present tense:

When did you [ms] arrive?	مَتَى حضرتَ؟
When will you [ms] travel?	مَتَى تسافر؟

أَيْنَ (*WHERE?*) is followed by **either a noun or a verb**:

> *Where is Ibrahim?* أَيْنَ إبراهيمُ؟

> *Where did you [ms] see my father?* أَيْنَ رأيتَ أَبي؟

كَيْفَ (*HOW?*) is used with **nouns and verbs**:

> *How are you [ms]?* كَيْفَ حالكَ؟

> *How did Najib travel?* كَيْفَ سافر نجيب؟

كَمْ (*HOW MANY?*): The noun that follows كَمْ is **singular, indefinite** and in the **accusative case**:

> *How many rooms are in the house?* كَمْ غرفةً في البيتِ؟

But **note** that if كَمْ is preceded by the preposition بِ or فِي then its noun can be in either the **accusative** or **genitive case**:

> *How much did the book cost you [ms]?*
>
> بِكَمْ ديناراً (دينارٍ) إشتريتَ الكتابَ؟
>
> [lit. How many dinars did you buy the book for?]

> *Seven dinars.* بِسبعةِ دَنانيرٍ.
>
> [بِ must also be in the answer]

In the next two instances the noun following كَمْ is in the **nominative case**:

> *What is the number of students?* كَمْ عددُ الطلابِ؟

> *What time is it?* كَمِ الساعةُ؟

> [lit. How much is the number of the students?]

كَمْ has another quite different use to express *"many, much"* and it does not require an answer. When used in this way كَمْ is referred to as كَمِ الخَبَرِيَّة *the informative*:

> *How wealthy you are!* كَمْ لَكَ مِنْ مالٍ!

> [lit. **How much** wealth you [ms] have!]

> *What a large number of books I have read* كَمْ كتابٍ قرأتُ!

The noun that follows كَمِ الْخَبَرِيّة is in the **genitive case** and may be a *singular* or a *broken plural*.

لِمَا and its shortened variant لِمَ and لِمَاذَا *(WHY?)*:

> *Why did they [mp] leave their homeland?*   لِمَاذَا غادروا وطنهم؟

> *Why were you [mp] absent?*   لِمَ كنتم غائبين؟

لِمَ in combination with لا or لَمْ introduces a **negative question** the answer to which requires a reason which in English can be supplied with *"because"*, e.g:

> *Why didn't you tell me?*   لِمَ لَمْ تخبرني؟

A number of interrogative pronouns may be preceded by prepositions. The two words may remain separate or they may merge and form a single word:

from where?	مِنْ أَيْنَ؟
in which?	فِي أَيٍّ؟
till when?	إِلَى مَتَى؟
to whom?	لِ + مَنْ = لِمَنْ؟
in which one?	بِ + مَنْ = بِمَنْ؟
in what?	بِ + مَاذَا = بِمَاذَا؟
about what?	عَنْ + مَاذَا = عَمَّاذَا؟

When مَا is *preceded by a preposition* the two words merge and the resulting word is usually written *without the alif*:

in what?	فِي + مَا = فِيمَ؟
in what? / with what?	بِ + مَا = بِمَ؟
for what? / on what?	عَلَى + مَا = عَلامَ؟
till when? / where to?	إِلَى + مَا = إِلامَ؟
about what?	عَنْ + مَا = عَمَّ؟ or عَمَّا؟
from what?	مِنْ + مَا = مِمَّ؟
why? / for what?	لِ + مَا = لِمَ؟
until when?	حَتَّى + مَا = حَتَّامَ؟

NEGATION AND PROHIBITION النَّفْي والنَّهْي

«لَا»

The particle «لَا» is of several types, each having its own special function:

1. As an equivalent to **no** and **not** (see Unit 23: Interrogatives).

2. When followed by the **present tense** it is used for:
    (a) **general negation**

    لاَ أَحِبُّ هذا الطعامَ *I don't like this food* [ever, at any time]

    (b) **denial**   لاَ أَفهمُهُ *I don't understand it*

Notes

  (i)   «لَا» may not negate the *past tense*. On the rare occasions when it is used with a verb in the *past tense*, it denotes a denial of wish, e.g. *God forbid!* لاَ سمحَ اللّه!

  (ii) One of the following words meaning **"never"** may be added to the sentence to emphasize the denial: مُطْلَقًا، قَطْعًا، بَتَاتًا، أَبَدًا

    لاَ يتأخر عَن الميعادِ أبدًا   *He is never late for an appointment*

3. «لَا» is used as a particle of prohibition (لاَ الناهِية). When «لَا» is followed by the **2nd person jussive**, it denotes a *negative command*, e.g. *Don't go* لاَ تذهبْ

4. When «لَا» is repeated in a sentence or after another negating particle, a series of denials or negations are expressed:

    There was no one in the house or in the garden

    مَا كان أحد في البيتِ ولا في البستانِ

    His wife does not know how to read and write
    [lit. ... does **not** know reading and **not** writing]

    زوجته لاَ تعرف القراءةَ ولاَ الكتابةَ

5. For **complete negation** لاَ النافِية لِلجِنْس:

No seeker of knowledge is disappointed   لاَ طالبَ علم خائبٌ

There is nothing here   لاَ شيءَ هنا

Case Endings

The *indefinite noun* or *adjective* following «لاَ» is in the **accusative case**, as shown in bold type in the above examples. **They do not take nunation.**

Notes

1. «لاَ» in the following phrases and others *does not necessarily* indicate a negative:

    no doubt   لاَ شَكَّ   especially, particularly   لاَ سِيَّمَا

2. «لاَ» may be prefixed by the preposition بِ. بِلاَ denotes **un-**, **-less** or **without**:

    senseless   بِلاَ معنًى   colourless   بِلاَ لون

«مَا»

«مَا» can be used to negate:

1. **The past tense**

    I did not write a letter   مَا كتبتُ رسالةً

    He did not come   مَا جاء

2. **The present tense**

    He is not reading [at the present moment]   مَا يقرأ

3. **A nominal sentence**

    No house is like my house   مَا بيتٌ كِبيتي

    Ali is not a writer   مَا علي كاتبًا

Case Endings

Normally «مَا» acts like لَيْسَ as its *subject* is in the **nominative case** and *its predicate* is in the **accusative case**. In many situations however, it loses its function, e.g. if its *predicate is preceded by* the exceptive particle إلاَّ.

«لَمْ»

«لَمْ» is used before the **present tense** giving the meaning of the **negated past**. In written Modern Standard Arabic this usage largely supersedes the use of «ما» + the past tense:

> *I did not travel* with them *[mp]* لَمْ أُسافِرْ معهم = ما سافَرْتُ معهم

> *They [mp] did not hear* the news

> لَمْ يَسْمَعُوا الأخبار = ما سَمِعُوا الأخبار

Note that the verb following «لَمْ» is in the **jussive mood (imperfect jussive)**. The use of «لَمْ» affects spelling of certain conjugations (see Unit 13: the Present Tense).

«غَيْر»

«غَيْر» is mainly used with **adjectives** to make the *opposite*, e.g. in-, un-, non-, **not**:

useful	مفيد	*not useful*	غَيْرُ مفيدٍ
important	مهمّ	*unimportant*	غَيْرُ مهمٍّ
*the believer and the **non-believer***			المؤمنُ وغَيْرُ المؤمنِ

«غَيْر» with *pronoun suffixes* becomes equivalent to "other":

> *them and others* هم وغَيْرُهم

Case Endings

«غَيْر» takes a vowel ending determined by its position in the sentence, while the adjective that follows it is *always* in the **genitive case**. This is shown by *nunation* when it is *indefinite* and كسرة when *definite*.

Note the change in meaning of غَيْر when combined with the following:
1. When «غَيْر» is preceded by the preposition مِنْ or بِ

> *without* مِنْ غَيْرِ

> *without* بِغَيْرِ

2. When «غَيْر» is preceded by the negating words لا or لَيْسَ

> *that is all, nothing else* لا غَيْرُ

> *that is all, nothing else* لَيْسَ غَيْرُ

3. When «غَيْر» is followed by the particle أَنَّ

except that غَيْر أَنَّ

4. When «غَيْر» is followed by the demonstrative pronoun ذَلِكَ

and the like, and so on غَيْرُ ذَلِكَ

«لَيْسَ»

«لَيْسَ» *not to be* occurs only in the **past tense** but it has a **present tense** meaning.

It is used to negate **nominal sentences** and means "**isn't**" when the *subject is definite*, and usually "**no**" when the *subject is indefinite*:

Salma isn't in the garden	لَيْسَتْ سلمى في الحديقة
*Samir isn't happy*****	لَيْسَ سمير سعيدًا*
*These is **no** child in the airplane*	لَيْسَ هناك طفل في الطائرة

* Note that سعيدًا is in the *accusative case* because it is the *predicate* of «لَيْسَ» which acts like كَانَ وَأَخَوَاتُهَا (see Unit 9: Nominal Sentences).

«لَيْسَ» is conjugated as follows:

	singular		dual			plural
I	لَسْتُ				*we*	لَسْنَا
you [ms]	لَسْتَ	*you [md]*	لَسْتُمَا	*you [mp]*	لَسْتُمْ
you [fs]	لَسْتِ	*you [fd]*	لَسْتُمَا	*you [fp]*	لَسْتُنَّ
he	لَيْسَ	*they [md]*	لَيْسَا	*they [mp]*	لَيْسُوا
she	لَيْسَتْ	*they [fd]*	لَيْسَتَا	*they [fp]*	لَسْنَ

«لَنْ»

«لَنْ» is used with the *subjunctive* to negate the **future**:

She won't come in the evening لَنْ تَحْضُرَ في المساءِ

*They [mp] **will not risk** their lives after that incident*

لَنْ يُجَازِفُوا* بحياتهم بعد تلك الحادثة

***Note** that conjugations which lose their final «نْ» with لَمْ also lose their «نْ» when used with لَنْ (see Unit 13: the Jussive and the Subjunctive).

«كَلَّا»

In classical Arabic «كَلَّا» simply means **"no"** or **"never"**.

«عَدِيم»

«عَدِيم» has the meaning: **-less, un-**. The noun following عديم is in the **genitive case**:

inanimate, lifeless   عَدِيمُ الحياةِ

*Pure water is **tasteless, colourless and odourless***

الماء النقيّ عَدِيمُ الطعمِ واللونِ والرائحةِ

«عَدَم»

«عَدَم» has the meaning: **non-, in-** and it precedes verbal nouns. عدم and the noun that follows it form a *construct phrase*:

non-existence   عَدَمُ الوجودِ

inability   عَدَمُ المقدرةِ

«بِدُونِ» and «دُونَ»

These two words are translated as **"without"**:

*coffee **with** sugar*   قهوة بِسكَّر

*coffee **without** sugar*   قهوة بِدُونِ سكَّر

*He reached this decision quickly and **without** hesitation*

وصل إلى هذا القرار بسرعة ودُونَ ترذُّد

Negation of Obligation

When **لا** precedes the verb يَجِبُ it is necessary the sense of obligation vanishes:

You must stay at home   يجب أنْ تبقى في البيت

It is not necessary for you to stay at home

لا يجب أنْ تبقى في البيت

When **لا** precedes the main verb of the sentence a negative obligation results:

You must not remain at home   يجب أنْ لا تبقى في البيت

Similarly عَدَم is used to express negative obligation when يَجِبُ is followed by a verbal noun:

No photography   يجب عدم التصوير

In speech لازم *must* in combination with **ما** is used to express lack of obligation and negative obligation:

(a) **ما** + **لازم** + present tense = lack of obligation

ما لازم تروح إلى المستشفى*You don't have to go to the hospital*

(b) **لازم** + **ما** + present tense = negative obligation

*You **must not** go to the hospital*   لازم ما تروح إلى المستشفى

CONJUNCTIONS حُرُوفُ العَطْفِ

Some of the more important conjunctions in Arabic are shown in the table below:

and	وَ	Used to join **sentences or nouns** and is considered as one word with the word that follows it. The following noun is in the **same case** as the preceding noun.
and so, then, so	فَ	Used to join **sentences or nouns** and is considered as one word with the word that follows it. *When used to join nouns* it denotes the sequence of their participation in the event/act. It can also imply cause and effect, a change or a development of events. The following noun is in the **same case** as the preceding noun.
then	ثُمَّ	It denotes a less immediate sequence than does «فَ»
or	أَوْ *	The noun following is in the **same case** as the preceding noun.
but, however, yet	بَلْ	When used after a *negative statement* it denotes: "**on the contrary**"

*The particle أَمْ, *or*, is always used in **alternative questions** (see Unit 23).

Examples:

I bought bread, cheese and meat   إِشتريتُ خبزًا وَجبنًا وَلحمًا

The patient [m] attended, then the nurse [m] and then the doctor [m]
حَضَرَ المريضُ فَالممرِّضُ فَالطبيبُ

*The sun appeared **and so** the temperature rose*

طلعت الشمسُ فَارتفعتْ درجةُ الحرارةِ

*I visit the capital once **or** twice a year*

أُسافرُ إلى العاصمةِ مرَّةً أَوْ مرّتينِ في السنةِ

*He received the message yesterday, **then** left the capital*

إسْتلمَ الرسالةَ أمس ثُمَّ غادرَ العاصمةَ

***He did not stay** in that job long, **but** he left after a short period*

لَمْ يَبْقَ في ذلك العملِ طويلاً بَلْ تَرَكَهُ بعد فترةٍ قصيرةٍ

In the last example, the verb يبقَ is the 3rd person masculine singular *present jussive of the indicative* يبقى

Alternative sentences, **either...or**, make use of إِمَّا... وَإِمَّا or إِمَّا ...أَوْ

Other words used as conjunctions include:

but	لَكِن
	[Note: dagger *alif*]
although	وَلَوْ
as for	أَمَّا
as, just as, as also	كَمَا
when, as, after	لَمَّا

Examples:

I am not hungry but thirsty

أنا لست جوعان ولَكِنّي عطشان

Ali is a diligent student, as for Zaid he is lazy

علي طالب مجتهد أَمَّا زيد فهو كسلان

He met many prominent persons of the town,
just as he met a number of bedouin sheikhs، قابل كثيرين من أعيان المدينة

كَمَا إنَّه قابل عددًا من شيوخ البدو

When we heard that news we rejoiced greatly

لَمَّا سمعنا ذلك الخبر فرحنا فرحًا عظيمًا

Compound Conjunctions

The particle أَنْ or مَا is often used after a preposition to form a compound conjunction. A compound conjunction is used to introduce a *verbal sentence*, whereas a preposition by itself *cannot precede a verb*.

Examples:

After I had eaten my breakfast I left the house

بَعْدَ أَنْ تناولتُ فطوري تركتُ البيت

Zaid left once he knew that his father's health was improving

سافر زيد بَعْدَمَا عرف أَنَّ صحة والده في تحسّن

He left quickly before his wife changed her mind

غادر بِسرعةٍ قَبْلَ أَنْ تغيّر زوجته رأيها

He had left the capital before the blockade started

ترك العاصمة قَبْلَمَا يبتدئ الحصار

When I was on my way home

عِنْدَمَا كنت في طريقي إلى بيتي

We stayed in London until the war ended

بقينا في لندن إلى أَنْ إنتهت الحرب

A discussion took place relating [in what relates]
to improving the present internal situation

جرى بحث فِيمَا يتعلّق
بتحسين الوضع الداخلي الحاضر

مَا is generally written attached to the preposition preceding it:

before	قَبْلَ + مَا = قَبْلَمَا	
while	بَيْنَ + مَا = بَيْنَمَا	
while, in what	فِي + مَا = فِيمَا	

VOCATIVE PARTICLES حُرُوفُ النِّداءِ

حروف النِّداء: يَا   أَ   آ   أَيُّها   أَيَّتُهَا

The vocative particles are used for addressing **a person by name** or **profession**. It is usual to use the particle before their name or title. (In archaic English there is a vestige of the vocative in phrases such as *"O wise one"* or *"O my lord"*).

يا is **the most frequently used vocative**. The other particles tend to be used in more formal Arabic. The noun following يا *cannot have the definite article.*

The noun following أَيُّها [m] and أَيَّتُهَا [f] *must* be defined by the definite article and therefore cannot be used with nouns in the construct state. These particles usually follow the particle يا, however يا can sometimes be omitted:

أَيّها السيّدات والسادة *Ladies and gentlemen*

Case Endings

The noun following the **vocative** (المُنَادَى) is in the **nominative case**, but *without nunation*, if it is (a) a proper noun consisting of one word; (b) a definite noun; or (c) an indefinite noun provided that the person addressed is present:

O Rashid!	يا رشيدُ
O student!	يا أَيُّها الطالبُ
O boy!	يا ولدُ
O doctor!	يا دُكتورُ

However, if the noun consists of **two words** (construct state) then the *first part* of the noun is in the **accusative case** and the *second part* is in the **genitive case**:

O Khair Allah!	آ خيرَ اللَّهِ
O housewives!	يا ربّاتِ البيوتِ

If the person addressed is absent or is in a group but has not been specified, then the noun will be in the **accusative case**:

O boy!   يا ولدًا

[lit.] *O treacherous one!*   يا غادرًا

Notes

1.   When addressing a person whose name you do not know use:

    يا سَيِّدي *for men* and يا سَيِّدتي *for women*

    When addressing a presumed educated person, as a form of respect use:

    يا أُستاذ *professor, teacher*

2.   The vocative particle يا may be used in exclamatory expressions. The noun following يا is prefixed by the preposition «لِ» which is changed to «لَ»:

    يا لَجمالِ الطبيعةِ! *O the beauty of nature!*

3.   يا is sometimes written without أَلِف when it is followed by a word which begins with an أَلِف:

    يا + أَيَّها = يٱيُّها

EXCEPTIVE SENTENCES أُسْلُوبُ الإِسْتِثْنَاءِ

The most common words (particles) to express *exceptions* are:

إِلاَّ   غَيْر   سِوَى   عَدَا   مَا عَدَا   خَلاَ   مَا خَلاَ

These words have the meaning **except, but** and are referred to as أَدوات المُسْتَثْنى. The main noun *preceding* the particle is referred to as الإِستثناء مِنهُ and the one *following* as المُسْتَثْنى.

Examples:

1. the engineers came except one

حضرَ المهندسونَ إِلاَّ واحدًا

Here the main noun, المهندسونَ *the engineers,* is the المُستثنى منه, and واحدًا *one* is the المستثنى.

2. Only one of the students failed

ما رسبَ من الطلابِ إِلاَّ طالبًا (طالبٍ)

3. Only children are in the house
[lit. None in the house **except** children]

لَيْسَ في الدَّارِ إِلاَّ أَطفالٌ

4. I have read Taha Hussain's books
***except* one [book]**

قرأتُ كتبَ طه حسين غَيْرَ كتابٍ

5. I haven't seen in my companion
[anything] ***except* truthfulness and loyalty**

مَا رأيتُ مِن رفيقي سِوَى الصدقِ والوفاءِ

*6. The friends came **except** Rashid*

أَقبل الأَصدقاء عَدَا رشيدًا (رشيدٍ)

*7. I like people **except** the wicked*

أُحبُّ الناسَ خَلاَ الخبيثَ (الخبيثِ)

*8. My colleagues took part in the stage play **except** Najib*

شارك في المسرحيّة زملائي مَا عَدَا نجيبًا

*9. I have read the book **except** one chapter.*

طالعتُ الكتابَ مَا خَلاَ فصلاً

Case Endings **(see numbered examples above)**

In constructions like **ex. 1** where the two elements of the exceptive sentence are present, the noun that follows إلاَّ (المُستثنى) is in the **accusative case.**

In **ex. 2** we have a ***negative sentence*** in which the noun preceding اِلَّا is mentioned. In such sentences the noun following اِلَّا can either be in the **accusative case** or it can be in the same case as the noun preceding اِلَّا.

If the sentence, as in **ex. 3**, *begins with a negative particle* and the main noun preceding اِلَّا is omitted, the case of the المُستثنى is governed by its position in the sentence regardless of اِلَّا.

In **ex. 4** and **5** a noun that follows غَيْر and سِوَى is in the *construct state* and therefore takes the **genitive case**.

In **ex. 6** and **7** a noun that follows عَدَا and خَلا can be in either the **accusative** or **genitive case**.

In **ex. 8** and **9** where عَدَا and خَلا are preceded by the negative particle ما, the noun following them will be in the **accusative case**.

CONDITIONAL SENTENCES أُسْلُوبُ الشَّرْطِ

The most common conjunctions used to express conditional sentences are:

مَنْ   إنْ   إذَا   لَوْ

These are referred to in Arabic as أَدوات الشَّرْط

إنْ، إذَا and لَوْ introduce "**if**" sentences and مَنْ introduces "**he who ...**" types of sentence.

Conditional (**if** and **then**) sentences consist of **three** elements: *a particle,* which comes at the beginning of the sentence, and **two verbs**:

> *If it snows **then** driving will be hazardous*

The *first verb* is referred to as فعْل الشَّرْط (condition "**if**") and the *second verb* (**answer** the main "**then**" clause) جواب الشّرط. The *first verb* stipulates a condition or a cause for the *second verb* to occur.

إنْ and إذَا are used to introduce conditional sentences *indicating an eventuality which is likely to occur.* In current usage, these two particles are often interchangeable.

لَوْ differs from the other conjunctions in that it introduces a hypothetical or impossible condition.

Examples:

> 1. *If I were a ruler* [then] *I would set the prisoner free*
>
> لَوْ كنتُ حاكمًا لأطلقتُ سراحَ السجين
>
> 2. *He who studies will succeed*
>
> مَنْ يدرسْ ينجحْ
>
> 3. *If you harm people* [then] *you will regret* [it]
>
> إنْ تُسِئْ إلى الناس تندمْ
>
> 4. *If ignorance **prevails*** [then] *the diseases **will increase***
>
> إذا سادَ الجهل كثرت الأمراض

*5. If you wish to succeed **do not** neglect your duty*

إِنْ أُردتَ النجاح فَلا تهملْ واجبك

Notes

In **ex. 1**, with لَوْ the *past tense* is used in both verbs. The second verb must be
  preceded by لَ.

In **ex. 2**, *the jussive mood* of the present tense is used in both verbs.

In **ex. 3**, *the jussive mood* of the present tense is used in both verbs.
  However the *past tense* can be used in both verbs or it can be used
  as either the first or the second verb in combination with the
  jussive. The different forms have little effect on meaning and *all
  express the present* or *the future*.

In **ex. 4**, إِذا is usually *followed by* the *past tense*, but *it indicates the present
  tense*.

In **ex. 5**, the second part of the conditional sentence is introduced by فَ
  because it is expressing prohibition. The second part of a
  conditional sentence is also introduced by فَ if it *expresses a
  wish or a command* or *if it is preceded by one of the particles* سَ,
  سَوْفَ, قَدْ, مَا *(not)*, or لَنْ

Other words which **introduce** conditional sentences are:

whatever	مَا
where	أَيْنَ
wherever	أَيْنَمَا
where	حَيْثُ
wherever	حَيْثُمَا
when	مَتَى
whenever	كُلَّمَا
whatever	مَهْمَا
whoever, whichever	أَيّ
how	كَيْفَ
however	كَيْفَمَا
if not, but for	لَوْلاَ
if not	إِلَّا

ARABIC NUMBERS العَدَدُ

The Arabic numerals are a difficult and complex topic, often varying from their written form in speech, and at times the grammar can appear quite illogical to the western mind. The **numerals** are written from **left to right**, e.g. 1999 is written as ١٩٩٩

Cardinal Numbers (spoken form) الأَعْدَادُ الأَصْلِيَّةُ

(a) Used in their "isolated form" for *counting* and *for telling the time in speech*;
(b) Used to express quantity when *followed by a noun*.

Numbers		الأرقام
0	صِفْر	٠
1	وَاحِد	١
2	إِثْنَيْن	٢
3	ثَلاثَة	٣
4	أَرْبَعَة	٤
5	خَمْسَة	٥
6	سِتَّة	٦
7	سَبْعَة	٧
8	ثَمَانِيَة	٨
9	تِسْعَة	٩
10	عَشَرَة	١٠
11	أَحَدَ عَشَرَ حِدَعْش	١١

168

12	إِثْنَا عَشَر إِثْنَعْش	١٢
13	ثَلاثَة عَشَر ثَلاتَعْش	١٣
14	أَرْبَعَة عَشَر أَرْبَعْتَعْش	١٤
15	خَمْسَة عَشَر خَمْستَعْش	١٥
16	سِتَّة عَشَر سِتَّعْش	١٦
17	سَبْعَة عَشَر سَبَعْتَعْش	١٧
18	ثَمانِيَة عَشَر ثَمَنْتَعْش	١٨
19	تِسْعَة عَشَر تِسَعْتَعْش	١٩

N.B. The *spoken form* of the numbers varies from one area to another. In the above table the numbers 11 - 9 are shown with the two most common variants.

Cardinal Numbers (written form) الأَعْدَادُ الأَصْلِيَّةُ

Take care in distinguishing the numbers ٢ and ٣ in *handwriting* as they are different from the printed form, i.e. **the handwritten 3 resembles the printed 2.**

	Notes	used with the Feminine	used with the Masculine	الأرقام
0			صِفْر	•
1	Not used as numerals is *spoken* Arabic*. These are used as **adjectives**, *follow* the counted noun and agree with it in gender. They are only used for emphasis.	إِحْدَى* وَاحِدَة	أَحَد* وَاحِد	١

* In this form أَحَد and إِحْدَى are used to express **"one of the"** as in:

one of the ministers [m]   أَحد الوزراء

one of the companies   إِحدى الشركات

2	These forms are used only when emphasis is required as the **dual noun** itself is used. When used they *follow* the noun.	إِثْنَتَان	إِثْنَانِ	٢
3	Numbers 3 - 10 form a group with the following characteristics: (a) **feminine ending** used with **masculine** counted noun; (b) **without feminine ending** used with **feminine** counted noun; (c) always followed by a noun in the **genitive plural**.	ثَلَاث	ثَلَاثَة	٣

4		أَرْبَع	أَرْبَعَة	٤
5		خَمْس	خَمْسَة	٥
6		سِتّ	سِتَّة	٦
7		سَبْع	سَبْعَة	٧
8	ثَمَانِي when followed by a counted noun.	ثَمَانٍ	ثَمَانِيَة	٨
9		تِسْع	تِسْعَة	٩
10		عَشْر	عَشَرَة	١٠
11	11 is **invariable**.	إِحْدَى عَشْرَة	أَحَدَ عَشَرَ	١١
12	The two elements of **12** are a **possessive construction**. The first element, being a dual, takes «ا» in the **nom.** and «ي» in the **acc. and gen.** cases. The second element is **invariable**.	إِثْنَتَا عَشْرَة	إِثْنَا عَشَرَ	١٢
13	The *10* part of the numbers *13 to 19* agrees with the counted noun in *gender*, but the *unit* part does not. These numbers are **invariable**.	ثَلَاثَ عَشْرَة	ثَلَاثَةَ عَشَرَ	١٣
14		أَرْبَعَ عَشْرَة	أَرْبَعَةَ عَشَرَ	١٤
15		خَمْسَ عَشْرَة	خَمْسَةَ عَشَرَ	١٥
16		سِتَّ عَشْرَة	سِتَّةَ عَشَرَ	١٦
17		سَبْعَ عَشْرَة	سَبْعَةَ عَشَرَ	١٧
18		ثَمَانِي عَشْرَة	ثَمَانِيَةَ عَشَرَ	١٨
19		تِسْعَ عَشْرَة	تِسْعَةَ عَشَرَ	١٩

20	The words for **20, 30, 40** etc. are used for both [m and f] counted nouns and are referred to as العُقود		عِشْرُونَ	٢٠
21	In the compound numbers **21 to 99** the *units come before the tens* and are connected by «وَ», e.g. one **and** twenty.	إحْدَى وَعِشْرُونَ	أَحَد وَعِشْرُونَ	٢١
22		إثْنَتَان وَعِشْرُونَ	إثْنَان وَعِشْرُونَ	٢٢
23		ثَلَاث وَعِشْرُونَ	ثَلَاثَة وَعِشْرُونَ	٢٣
100	**Note** the irregular spelling. The «ا» is not pronounced. Both forms of the word are used and have the same pronunciation. **100** and its multiples* are used for both [m and f] counted nouns.		مِئَة or مِائَة	١٠٠
200	Spoken dialects use ـَيْن ending.		مِئَتَانِ or مِائَتَانِ	٢٠٠
300 . . . 900	These numbers are formed from the numbers **3-9** in the form used for [f] nouns followed by مئة/مائة in a *construct state*. May be written as a single word or two words.		ثَلَاثَمِئَةٍ or ثَلَاث مِائَةٍ	٣٠٠ . . . ٩٠٠

* The plural of مائة is مئات which is used for **hundreds** in an indefinite sense:

hundreds of women and men   مئات من النساء والرجال

1,000	Used for both [m and f] counted nouns.	أَلْف	١٠٠٠
2,000	Spoken dialects use يْن ending.	أَلْفَانِ	٢٠٠٠
5,000	Note the plural spellings: آلاف or أُلوف*	خَمْسَة آلافٍ	٥٠٠٠
100,000		مِئَة أَلْفٍ	١٠٠٠٠٠
1,000,000		مَلْيُون	١٠٠٠٠٠٠
2,000,000	Spoken dialects use يْن ending.	مَلْيُونَانِ	٢٠٠٠٠٠٠
3,000,000	**Note** the plural spelling which is a diptote.	ثَلاثَة مَلايِين	٣٠٠٠٠٠٠
1 billion	**1,000,000,000**	مِلْيَار	(١٠٠٠٠٠٠٠٠٠)

*أُلُوف which is used for **thousands** in an indefinite sense:

tens of thousands   عشرات الأُلوف

The following points should be noted when **writing compound numbers in words**:

1. *Two or more* numbers are joined by و *and.*
2. The *dual form* of the number is used with: **2, 200, 2,000** and **2 million** and takes the ending «ان» when in the **nominative case** and «يْنَ» in the **accusative** and **genitive cases**. This also applies to the **2** if it is the unit part of a compound number.
   Spoken dialects use the «يْنَ» ending form.
3. The *tens* are declined as (smp) with «ونَ» in the **nominative case** and with «ينَ» in the **accusative** and **genitive cases**. Spoken dialects use the «ينَ» ending form.
4. The numbers **300 - 900** are written as **one word** (although writing them as two words is also used).
5. **Note** the word order in compound numbers:
   millions, thousands, hundreds, *units and tens.*

6. The numerals **11 - 99** inclusive have their counted noun in the *indefinite accusative singular* having the nunation -an.

7. Arabic considers «مـائـة» as being the first part of a *possessive construction* in «مائة كتاب», therefore the «ة» ending is pronounced as a «ت».

8. مائة, ألف and مَلْيُون and their multiples are followed by an *indefinite singular noun* in the **genitive case**.

Ordinal Numbers الأَعْدَادُ التَّرْتِيبِيَّةُ

Ordinal numbers may either *precede* or *follow* the noun.

When the ordinal comes **before** the noun, both the ordinal and the noun are used *without* the article and the *masculine form* of the ordinal is used regardless of the gender of the noun.

When the ordinal **follows** the noun, the most common use is when both noun and ordinal are *definite*. The ordinal here is used as an adjective and must agree in gender and case with the noun.

Numbers	Notes	used with the Feminine	used with the Masculine
1st		الأُولى	الأَوَّل
2nd		الثَّانِيَة	الثَّانِي
3rd	The ordinal numbers **3rd-10th** are of the pattern فَاعِل	الثَّالِثَة	الثَّالِث
4th		الرَّابِعَة	الرَّابِع
5th		الخَامِسَة	الخَامِس
6th	**Note** the change of root.	السَّادِسَة	السَّادِس
7th		السَّابِعَة	السَّابِع
8th		الثَّامِنَة	الثَّامِن

9th		التَّاسِعَة	التَّاسِع
10th		العَاشِرَة	العَاشِر
11th	The ordinal numbers 11th-19th are *invariable*.	الحَادِيَة عَشَرَة	الحَادِي عَشَرَ
12th		الثَّانِيَة عَشَرَة	الثَّانِي عَشَرَ
13th		الثَّالِثَة عَشَرَة	الثَّالِثَ عَشَرَ
20th	For the **tens** the **cardinal form** is used.		العِشْرُونَ العِشْرِين -in speech
21st 31st 41st		الحَادِيَة والعِشْرُونَ	الحَادِي والعِشْرُونَ
25th	For the **tens** the **cardinal form** is used, but if this is preceded by a **unit** then the **unit** is in the **ordinal form**.	الخَامِسَةُ والعِشْرُونَ	الخَامِسُ والعِشْرُونَ

N.B. *Once* مَرَّة واحدةً or مَرَّة   *Twice* مَرَّتَيْنِ   *Three times* ثَلاث مَرَّاتٍ

Examples:

1 book	كتابٌ واحدٌ or كتابٌ
1 car	سيّارةٌ واحدةٌ or سيّارةٌ
2 books	كتابانِ
3 books	ثلاثةُ كُتُبٍ
4 cars	أربعُ سيّاراتٍ
4 teachers [m]	أربعةُ مدرِّسينَ
11 books	أحَدَ عَشَرَ كِتَابًا
13 cars	ثلاثَ عَشَرَة سيّارةً
20 teachers [m]	عشرونَ مدرِّسًا

175

20 teachers [f]	عِشرونَ مُدرِّسَةً
36 books	سِتَّةٌ وثلاثونَ كتابًا
43 cars	ثلاثٌ وأَربعونَ سيّارةً
100 books	مِئَةُ كتابٍ
101 books	مِئَةٌ وكتابٌ
202 books	مِئتانِ وكتابانِ
303 books	ثلاثُمِئةٍ وثلاثةُ كتبٍ
415 cars	أَربعُمئةٍ وخمسَ عشْرةَ سيّارةً
500 books	خمسُمائةِ كتابٍ
1,000 books	أَلفُ كتابٍ
2,000 books	أَلفا كتابٍ

[the **dual** governed by a *genitive* loses its final «نْ»]

5,000 books	خمسةُ آلافِ كتابٍ
the 1st lesson	الدرسُ الأَوَّلُ
the 1st student [f]	الطالبةُ الأُولى
the 8th floor	الطابقُ الثامِنُ

Summary

1. A noun *directly preceded* by the numbers **3 - 10** is always in its *plural form*.
2. The plural form of the noun is also used if it is *preceded* by the numbers **3 - 9** regardless of what other number may occur before them, i.e. 104, 2006 etc.
3. A *singular form* of the noun is used in **all** other situations.

Fractions كُسُور

	Plural	Singular
half	أَنْصَاف	نِصْف
third	أَثْلاث	ثُلْث

quarter	أَرْبَاع	رُبْع
fifth	أَخْمَاس	خُمْس
sixth	أَسْدَاس	سُدْس
seventh	أَسْبَاع	سُبْع
eighth	أَثْمَان	ثُمْن
ninth	أَتْسَاع	تُسْع
tenth	أَعْشَار or عُشُور	عُشْر

plus + زَائِد minus – نَاقِص multiplied by × فِي divided by ÷ عَلى

equals = يُسَاوِي per cent % بالمئة or في المئة 20% = ٪٢٠

14,563 is written as: أَربعةَ عشَرَ ألفًا وخمسُمائةٍ وثلاثةٌ وستّونَ or ١٤٥٦٣

year عام or سنة

The year 1999 is written as: سنة ألف وتسعمئة وتسع وتسعين or

عام ألف وتسعمئة وتسعة وتسعين or

classical Arabic سنة تسع وتسعين وتسعمئة وألف

19/5/1999 is written as: ١٩ أيار ١٩٩٩ or ١٩٩٩/٥/١٩

The word رَقْم *numeral* is used for **telephone numbers, house numbers,** etc.

The word عَدَد *quantity* is used for describing **amounts.**

بِضْع، نَيِّف، كَذَا

These words are used specifically when the exact number is not stated.

بِضْع and بِضْعَة *some, a few, several*

Note: Do not confuse these two words with بَعْض *some.*

177

These stand for an unspecified number from **3 - 10** and follow their perverted gender pattern, i.e. بِضْع is used for *feminine nouns* and بِضْعَة is used for *masculine nouns*. They also govern the counted noun grammatically in the same way that these numbers do when used as single numbers or in compound numbers:

بِضْعَةُ أَيَّام *some days*

بِضْعُ نِساءٍ *a few women*

*We have covered a distance estimated to be **some thirty miles***

قطعنا مسافةً تُقَدَّر بِبِضْعَةٍ وثلاثِينَ مِيلاً

نَيِّف *in excess of*

نَيِّف is used for an indefinite number **over 10** and denotes a number that lies between **a 10** and the **following 10**. Its counted noun is **singular** and is in the **accusative case**. It is used for both *masculine* and *feminine* nouns:

thirty odd نَيِّفٌ وَثَلاثُونَ

fifty or more students [mp] نَيِّفٌ وخمسونَ طالبًا

كَذَا *so many* or *so much*

This word can be used to give impression of *less or more* as intended by the speaker:

[lit.] *Her age is **so and so** many years* عمرها كَذَا سنواتٍ

[lit.] ***So and so** many dinars* كَذَا وَكَذَا دينارًا

Telling the Time

Telling the time in Arabic can be confusing as there are differences between the *colloquial* and *written* forms.

In the *written* form **ordinal numbers** are used, but the *colloquial* form uses **cardinal numbers** (note the exception with one o'clock).

It is not necessary to use the word for *"minute(s)"* (دَقَائِق) دَقِيقَة when telling the time in Arabic:

What time is it?	كَمِ الساعةُ؟	*What time is it?*	الساعةُ كَمْ؟
The time is ...	الساعة...	*less, minus*	إلاّ
and	وَ	*second(s)*	ثانية (ثوانٍ)
moment(s), instant	لحظة (ات)	*in a moment*	في لحظة
at once, immediately	حالاً	*half*	نِصْف (نصّ .colloq)
third	ثُلْث	*quarter*	رُبع

Colloquial Form		**Written Form**
الساعة	*hour/o'clock*	الساعة
واحدة	*one o'clock*	الواحدة
ثنتين	*two o'clock*	الثانية
ثلاثة	*three o'clock*	الثالثة
أربعة	*four o'clock*	الرابعة
خمسة	*five o'clock*	الخامسة
ستّة	*six o'clock*	السادسة
سبعة	*seven o'clock*	السابعة
ثمانية	*eight o'clock*	الثامنة
تسعة	*nine o'clock*	التاسعة
عشرة	*ten o'clock*	العاشرة
حدعش	*eleven o'clock*	الحادية عشرة
إثنعش	*twelve o'clock*	الثانية عشرة
واحدة وخمسة	*1:05*	الواحدة وخمس دقائق
ثنتين وعشرة	*2:10*	الثانية وعشر دقائق
ثلاثة وربع	*3:15*	الثالثة والربع

أربعة وثلث	4:20	الرابعة والثلث
خمسة ونصّ إلاّ خمسة	5:25	الخامسة والنصف إلاّ خمس دقائق
ستّة ونصّ	6:30	السادسة والنصف
سبعة ونصّ وخمسة	7:35	الثامنة إلاّ خمس وعشرين دقيقة
تسعة إلاّ ثلث	8:40	التاسعة إلاّ ثلثًا
عشرة إلاّ ربع	9:45	العاشرة إلاّ ربعًا
احدعش إلاّ عشرة	10:50	الحادية عشرة إلاّ عشر دقائق
إثنعش إلاّ خمسة	11:55	الثانية عشرة إلاّ خمس دقائق
إثنعش	12:00	الثانية عشرة
عشرة الصبّاح (صباحًا)	10:00 am	العاشرة الصباح (صباحًا)
الظهر (ظهرًا)	12:00 noon	الظهر (ظهرًا)
ثنتين بعد الظّهر	2:00 pm	الثانية بعد الظّهر
سبعة المساء (مساءً)	7:00 pm	السابعة المساء (مساءً)
مُنتصف الليل or نصّ الليل	midnight	مُنتصف الليل or نصف الليل

Note: In Arabic, the days of the week closely follow the numbers 1-7 with the exception of *Friday* (see Appendix 3: ***Days of the Week and Months of the Year***).

MEMBERS OF THE ARAB LEAGUE جَامِعَةُ الدُّوَلِ العَرَبِيَّةِ

العاصمة	Capital	البلد	Country
الجزائر	Algiers	الجزائر	Algeria
المنامة	Manama	البحرين	Bahrain
موروني	Moroni	جزر القمر	Comoros
جيبوتي	Djibouti	جيبوتي	Djibouti
القاهرة	Cairo	مصر	Egypt
بغداد	Baghdad	العراق	Iraq
عمَّان	Amman	الأردن	Jordan
الكويت	Kuwait City	الكويت	Kuwait
بيروت	Beirut	لبنان	Lebanon
طرابلس	Tripoli	ليبيا	Libya
نواكشوط	Nouakchott	موريتانيا	Mauritania
الرباط	Rabat	المغرب	Morocco
مسقط	Musqat	عُمان	Oman
القدس*	Jerusalem*	فلسطين	Palestine
دوحة	Doha	قطر	Qatar
الرياض	Riyadh	المملكة العربية السعودية	Kingdom of Saudi Arabia

* In 1988 the Palestine National Council decreed that Jerusalem would be the capital of any independent Palestinian state. However, the final status of Jerusalem remains subject to negotiation in the context of the Oslo Agreement of 1995.

مقديشو	Mogadishu	الصومال	Somalia
الخرطوم	Khartoum	السودان	Sudan
دمشق	Damascus	سوريا	Syria
تونس	Tunis	تونس	Tunisia
أبو ظبي	Abu Dhabi	الإمارات العربية المتّحدة	United Arab Emirates:
		أبو ظبي	*Abu Dhabi*
		عجمان	*Ajman*
		دبيّ	*Dubai*
		الفجيرة	*Fujairah*
		رأس الخيمة	*Ras al-Khaimah*
		الشارقة	*Sharjah*
		أمّ القيوين	*Umm al-Qaiwain*
صنعاء	San'a	اليمن	Yemen

ARAB NAMES الأَسْمَاءُ العَرَبِيَّةُ

There is a logical structure to seemingly incomprehensible Arab names. In many ways they are more logical than in the West.

The names of most Arabs are constructed of three, but occasionally of four parts. Consider a man whose name is:

Khalid Ali al-Fulani خالد علي الفلاني

Khalid is the man's first name, and this is what he is called by his friends and family. *Ali* is his father's first name and *al-Fulani* is the family's name. *Khalid's* sister, whose first name is *Fatima,* would call herself:

Fatima Ali al-Fulani فاطمة علي الفلاني

All the siblings of that family would share the middle name, that of their **father's first name.**

Women *retain* their maiden name after marriage.

When the name consists of four parts, the two middle names are the first names of the father and the grandfather respectively.

Frequently we come across the words *bin* بن and *ibn* إبن *(the son of)* as part of the name. Consider a man whose name is:

Khalid bin Ahmad al-Fulani خالد بن أحمد الفلاني

His first name is *Khalid* and his father's first name is *Ahmad.*

The noun إبن drops its *alif* when it comes between the name of the son and that of the father.

The noun *banu/bani* بنو/بني is the plural of *bin* and often precedes the name of a clan or tribe:

the family of Hashim/the bani Hashim بني هاشم

In Arabic an alternative way of referring to the family of *Hashim* is to add the letter «ي» at the end of the name. Thus *Hashim* becomes *Hashimi:*

هاشمي

These names are often prefixed by *al-*, e.g. *al-Ayoubi* الأيوبي. Names of this kind, when they are of historical significance, are often written in western literature with an added **-d** at the end of the name. Thus *al-Ayoubi* الأيوبي is written as *Ayoubid*.

The word آل preceding the last part of the name denotes *"the clan of"*.

The word *abd* عبد *(the slave or servant)* often appears in men's names. It is the first part of a **compound** name, the second part of which is one of the ninety-nine divine attributes. The following are a few of the names which belong to this group and their meanings:

Servant of God	عبد الله
Servant of the Merciful	عبد الرحمن
Servant of the Almighty	عبد العزيز
Servant of the Powerful	عبد القادر
Servant of the Generous	عبد الكريم
Servant of the One	عبد الواحد

Other compound names used as **first names** include:

khair allah	خير الله
sa'd allah	سعد الله
maal allah	مال الله
jaad allah	جاد الله
izz id-diin	عزّ الدين
khair id-diin	خير الدين
nuur id-diin	نور الدين

It is also customary to call a man or a woman after the name of his or her first-born son or daughter. Thus the father and mother of *Hassan* would be called:

Abu Hassan [father]	أبو حسن
Umm Hassan [mother]	أمّ حسن

Family names may originate from trades or professions:

the butcher	الجزّار
the tailor	الخيّاط
the goldsmith	الصائغ
the gardener	البستاني
the merchant	التاجر

Alternatively the family name may originate from a place name:

| the man from Aleppo | الحلبي |
| the man from Persia | الفارسي |

Sometimes a name is preceded by *Haj* حاج. This is an honorific title of one who has performed the pilgimage to Mecca.

Listed below is a selection of common Arabic names. As in the West, there are names that are exclusively male or female. Some names are common to both genders. However there are certain masculine names that, with the addition of the suffix «ة», become female names (some of these can be seen in the table below).

Men's names + ة = Women's names	both Men and Women	Women only	Men only
نجيب (ة)	صباح	خديجة	محمّد
سمير (ة)	جنان	عائشة	عُمر
جميل (ة)	نور	فاطمة	قيس
منير (ة)	بهاء	زينب	إبراهيم
مفيد (ة)	رجاء	سعاد	أحمد
أمين (ة)	نجاح	ليلى	عثمان
نجم (ة)	صفاء	بلقيس	مصطفى
باسم (ة)	إيمان	خنساء	زيد
فوزي (ة)	إلهام	مريم	إسماعيل

DAYS OF THE WEEK أَيَّامُ الأُسْبُوعِ

Sunday	يَوْم الأَحَد
Monday	يَوْم الإِثْنَيْنِ
Tuesday	يَوْم الثَّلاثَاء
Wednesday	يَوْمَ الأَرْبَعَاء
Thursday	يَوْم الخَميس
Friday [holy day and official rest day]	يَوْم الجُمْعَة
Saturday	يَوْم السَّبْت

Sometimes the days are written without the word يوم

Note: In Arabic *"on Wednesday morning"* becomes *"in Wednesday morning"*: في صباح يوم الأربعاء

Calendar Conversions

To calculate conversions from the **Gregorian calendar (G)** to the **Islamic calendar (H)** use the formula:

   G = H + 622 − (H ÷ 33) e.g. using this formula 1991 AD gives AH 1412.

To calculate conversions from the **Islamic calendar (H)** to the **Gregorian calendar (G)** use the formula:

   H = 1.031 (G − 622) e.g. using this formula AH 1400 gives 1979 AD.

N.B. For those who are mathematically inclined either of the above formulae can be used for these conversions.

MONTHS OF THE YEAR أَشْهُرُ السَّنَةِ

الأَشْهُر المِيلادِيَّة	الأَشْهُر الهِجْرِيَّة	الأَشْهُر العَرَبِيَّة	الأَشْهُر الغَرْبِيَّة
January	المُحَرَّم	كَانُون الثَّانِي	يَنَايِر
February	صَفَر	شُبَاط	فَبْرَايِر
March	رَبِيع الأَوَّل	آذَار	مَارْس
April	رَبِيع الثَّانِي	نَيْسَان	أَبْرِيل
May	جُمَادَى الأُولَى	أَيَّار	مَايُو
June	جُمَادَى الآخِرَة	حَزِيرَان	يُونِيُو
July	رَجَب	تَمُوز	يُولِيُو
August	شَعْبَان	آب	أَغُسْطُس
September	رَمَضَان	أَيْلُول	سَبْتَمْبِر
October	شَوَّال	تِشْرِين الأَوَّل	أُكْتُوبِر
November	ذُو القَعْدَة	تِشْرِين الثَّانِي	نُوفَمْبِر
December	ذُو الحِجَّة	كَانُون الأَوَّل	دِيسَمْبِر
Gregorian	**Lunar** (354 days) These months do not coincide with the Gregorian calendar.	**Gregorian** (as used in the eastern Arab world)	**Gregorian** (transliterated from the Roman Christian calendar)

The Muslim era dates from الهجرة, *the Flight* or *Emigration* (28th June 622 AD), when the Prophet Muhammad and his companions left Mecca for Medina. The Islamic year uses lunar months which have 29 and 30 days alternately, and is roughly 11 days shorter than the solar year.

To denote the **Islamic year** in English, **AH** is used before the year, e.g. **AH 1467**. In Arabic the *initial* form of the leter *haa'* is used after the year.

AD is expressed in Arabic by the letter «م» (an abbreviation of the word ميلادِيّة) used after the year, e.g. م ١٤٦٧.

ARABIC INDEX

Words are arranged alphabetically without regard to roots.

ENGLISH INDEX